HOMEMADE HEALTHY DOG FOOD GUIDE

Discover the science behind nutritional solutions, tailored to your dog's health at every stage of life, for chronic or pathological conditions, and for breed-specific needs

Susan Swanson

Your Additional Content Is Waiting for You!

To request additional content or upcoming publications, contact the author directly at the following email address: *susan.dog.food@ltpublishing.net*

Here is what you will receive:

- The **AUDIOBOOK** of the book

- A **FULL-COLOR PDF** version of the book

- An introductory chapter on basic training and how to solve your dog's biggest behavior problems

- A table of all toxic foods for dogs

- A special, balanced, and nutritious recipe written by a veterinary nutritionist to try right away

- A **Q&A** with our authors

- Get early access to a preview of our other canine publications

Dedication

I dedicate this book to all my dogs.

If even a small part of what you have taught me is useful to our readers, then I will have done a good job.

Thank you, guys.

Contents

Warnings

When it comes to pet food and homemade meals, it's important to provide warnings and recommendations to ensure the safety and well-being of our beloved pets.

Here are some precautions to consider:

- **Consult a Professional:** Before making any significant changes to your dog's diet, always consult a professional veterinarian or veterinary nutritionist. This is the first rule.

- **Gradual Introduction:** When introducing a new diet or food, do so gradually. Mixing the new food with the old in increasing proportions over a week can help with the transition from industrial to homemade meals.

- **Fresh Water Access:** Always ensure that your dog has access to fresh, clean water, especially when introducing new foods that may increase thirst.

- **Individual Needs:** Every dog is unique. What works for one may not work for another. Monitor your dog's response to any diet changes and adjust accordingly.

- **Storage and Freshness:** Homemade meals don't have the preservatives found in commercial dog foods, so they can deteriorate faster. Keep them in the fridge and consume them within a set time frame (usually 3–4 days) to ensure freshness.

- **Supplements:** If certain nutrients are difficult to include in homemade meals, consider adding dog-friendly supplements. This could include things like fish oil for Omega-3 fatty acids.

- **Portion Control:** Pay attention to portion sizes. Overfeeding can be just as harmful as underfeeding. Adjust the amount based on your dog's size, activity level, and specific nutritional needs.

The job of a veterinary nutritionist is to formulate individual prescriptions based on the patient's medical history and examination reports. Regular veterinary check-ups are essential to monitor overall health and meet your dog's nutritional needs, even if you're feeding what you believe to be a nutritious and healthy diet. Never forget this crucial step.

Who Is This Book For?

This book was born out of a love for dogs and a passion for understanding their nutritional needs. My personal experience with all my dogs, extensive documentation, and the advice of expert veterinary nutritionists I have met have guided the writing of this book. It is more than just a collection of recipes; it is a guide to feeding your dog at every meal, and it is your ally in making sure your furry friend gets the best.

As you read these words, know that you have already taken a step towards a healthier and happier life for your canine companion. Let's examine the target audience for this book:

- **Health-Conscious Dog Owners:** For those who know how important a dog's diet is to its well-being, here you will find advice for all aspects of your dog's health, from a shiny coat to strong bones, from energetic days to peaceful nights. You can adapt homemade meals for puppies, adults, and senior dogs, ensuring they receive the right nutrition at every stage of their lives.

- **New Dog Owners:** If you are a new dog parent and feel lost in the sea of commercial dog food choices, this book is your beacon of reference. Together, we will cover the basics of dog nutrition and make the process of preparing meals simple and enjoyable. We have designed all recipes to be both affordable and nutritious, making them ideal for initiating a rewarding and healthy journey for your dog.

- **Experienced Dog Owners:** For those who have been on this journey for some time, this book promises to bring new flavors to your dog's diet. Food boredom is not just a human problem; even our four-legged friends appreciate a change of pace! Here, you'll find tips that will breathe new life into their meals and ensure they're always excited about what's in their bowl.

- **Dog Owners with Special Dietary Requirements:** Dogs, like people, can have special health needs and allergies. This book pays special attention to these dogs. Whether it's low-fat diets for weight management, grain-free options for allergies, or nutrient-rich meals for specific health conditions, you'll find guidance to meet all these needs.

- **The Environmentally and Budget-Conscious:** Homemade dog food is not only good for your dog, but it is also good for the planet and your wallet. By choosing to prepare your dog's meals at home, you can reduce packaging waste and control the quality of the ingredients. This book also provides tips on how to prepare the right amount of food for your dog's needs (based on age, energy expenditure, and health) while saving time and money and helping the environment.

I know some of the topics may seem boring or repetitive, but I wanted to explore all these questions thoroughly. Each section of this book contains a detailed bibliography for further reading. You can improve your pet's quality of life and strengthen your relationship with them by paying attention to their special needs, sourcing quality ingredients, and preparing balanced meals at home.

After all, no one likes to go to the doctor or a nutritionist, and dogs are no different. After reading this book, you will not only fully understand the impact of nutrition on your dog's health, but you will also have a useful scientific basis for better understanding your veterinarian's instructions.

Please do not hesitate to contact me at *authors@ltpublishing.net*. Your opinions and comments are not only welcome but greatly appreciated, as they help me to learn and improve. I look forward to hearing from you and your furry friends.

Enjoy your meal!

Introduction

When I faced the problem of how to feed my dogs properly, I found that there were no satisfactory books on the subject. I encountered books with lists of elaborate recipes that seemed more appropriate for humans than for dogs.

A book with a hundred or more dog recipes makes no sense; cooking for your dog should be simple, natural, and nutritious. I even found birthday cakes and Christmas recipes! This risks humanizing them and harming their health. Also, my dogs are all different, and what seemed to make one feel good or happy didn't work for another.

In short, I had a lot of confusion in my head and few clear ideas. I began studying, doing my own research, and talking to experienced breeders, veterinarians, and veterinary nutritionists. My research led to the creation of this book. I really hope it can help you get your dog healthy.

A Historical Perspective on Canine Nutrition

But let's start at the beginning, at the dawn of human history. It is important to remember that dogs were the first domesticated animals kept as pets by humans [1]. Because they were considered members of the tribe, they fed them the same food as their masters [2], both for convenience and because there was nothing else to eat. I can't imagine a caveman preparing two different meals, one for himself and one for his dog!

If a primitive man could get food, he would eat it that day, as would his dog; otherwise, they would both fast for days. Both, having experienced food shortages, were not too fussy. The history of the dog explains why it eats whatever comes its way, immediately and without being picky. Dogs can eat both animal and plant foods, but they prefer nutritious foods such as meat and fresh vegetables [3].

Of course, packaged treats and sweets did not exist in prehistoric times. If you get the impression that your dog is ready to dive into a treat instead of meat and vegetables, it's because he's learned it from us. In nature, dogs (and even humans) have no way of knowing the taste of refined sugar, ice cream, or chocolate!

After exploring the historical approach to canine nutrition, it's important to see how these practices have evolved with scientific advancement. Today, the science of canine nutrition provides us with opportunities to customize our dogs' diets like never before.

Canine Nutrition: Modern Challenges

Fortunately, we are not in prehistoric times, and in most countries, neither we nor our dogs have to endure hunger and deprivation. On the contrary, today there is an abundance of readily available food in the countries we call civilized. Today, we also know that this readily available food (primarily raw animal by-products) is the root cause of many of the world's most serious public health, animal welfare, and food safety problems.

Nowadays, it is well known that dog owners consider them family members and ideal companions for lonely people. They are also concerned about the health of their dogs and want to provide them with the best possible nutrition. We have also seen an increase in the demand for organic food in recent years, leading to a greater focus on this type of dog food.

Many dog owners are switching from buying commercial dog food to making homemade dog food that is organic, tasty, and nutritionally sound [4]. There is also a strong trend toward choosing food suitable for human consumption, as if human and dog food are interchangeable.

Setting the Record Straight

For all these reasons, I believe it's time to rectify the situation. Nutrition is one of the most important variables in a dog's overall health. Providing your dog with proper nutrition is essential for his development, vitality, and survival.

In this comprehensive guide, we will discuss the importance of proper nutrition for a dog's overall health, review the basic characteristics of dog food, and explore the benefits of making your own dog food, which every responsible dog owner should be aware of. While considering the broad spectrum of canine nutritional needs, let us now focus on the specific requirements of dogs based on their age, breed, and activity level.

An Overview of a Dog's Nutritional Needs

Before we discuss the importance of dog food, we must first understand the different nutritional needs of dogs. A proper dog diet must be rich in essential nutrients, but what does that mean? The diet must supply essential nutrients, substances that the dog's body cannot produce in sufficient amounts on its own. Dogs, like humans, need a variety of food groups to maintain optimal health. These include certain vitamins, minerals, fatty acids, and amino acids, all crucial for maintaining their health. There are six main categories into which these nutrients fall:

1. **Proteins:** Proteins are the basic building blocks of life. They are essential for development, maturation, and overall well-being. Dogs need high-quality animal-based proteins, such as those found in fish and meat [5].

2. **Carbohydrates:** Carbohydrates provide energy for your dog. Although dogs are omnivores, they do not need as many carbohydrates as humans, but only a modest amount. A healthy dog diet may include carbohydrates from foods such as grains, vegetables, and fruits [6]. Dietary fibers, found in foods like vegetables and whole grains, play a critical role in regulating a dog's digestion. They help maintain regular bowel movements and support good intestinal microbiota health.

3. **Fats:** Fats provide a rich source of energy and are necessary for fat-soluble vitamin absorption. They also promote the health of your dog's skin and coat. For dogs, healthy fats from sources such as beef and fish are good [7].

4. **Vitamins:** Vitamins A, B, C, D, E, and K are essential for dogs. Each vitamin has a specific purpose, such as immune support, healthy skin, and overall vitality [8].

5. **Minerals:** Minerals like calcium, phosphorus, potassium, and salt are essential for bones, teeth, and electrolyte balance [9].

6. **Water:** Your dog needs water, the most important nutrient, for every biological process, from metabolism to temperature regulation.

The Science Behind Nutritional Needs

Dogs' nutritional requirements are not universal. Age, breed, size, exercise level, and underlying health concerns all impact their dietary demands. Scientific studies have shed light on these issues, allowing us to tailor meals to individual pets.

1. **Nutrition for Every Stage of Life:** Dogs go through different stages of life, each with unique nutritional needs. For example, puppies need a high-protein, calcium-rich diet to support their rapid growth, while older dogs benefit from a lower-calorie diet to prevent obesity and joint problems [10].

2. **Size and Breed Considerations:** Different breeds and sizes of dogs have different metabolisms and sensitivities to certain health conditions. For example, smaller breeds may be more susceptible to dental disease, while larger breeds may be more prone to joint problems [11]. It is important to tailor the diet to these unique needs.

3. **Level of Activity:** A dog's level of activity has a significant impact on its caloric needs. To maintain their energy expenditure [12], energetic or athletic breeds require more calories.

The Benefits of a Balanced Dog Diet

Now that we know what elements dogs need. Let's look a little closer at why proper nutrition is so important for them:

- **Overall Well-Being:** A healthy diet is the cornerstone of your dog's health. It helps maintain a healthy body weight, promotes good physiology, and lowers the risk of chronic diseases.

- **Energy Levels:** Proper nutrition ensures dogs have the energy they need for fun, sports, and mental engagement. Dogs who are energetic are happy.

- **Healthy Weight Control:** Obesity is a major problem in the canine world, just as it is in humans. Feeding your dog the right portion sizes and nutritious foods will help maintain a healthy weight, reducing the risk of joint disease, diabetes, and heart problems.

- **Strong Immune System:** Proper nutrition helps boost your dog's immune response, making them more resistant to disease and infection.

- **Healthy Skin and Coat:** High-quality protein and essential fatty acids support both healthy skin and a shiny coat. This not only looks fantastic, but it also protects against environmental pollutants.

- **Digestive Health:** A well-balanced diet high in fiber helps reduce the risk of digestive problems such as diarrhea and constipation.

- **Longevity:** Well-nourished dogs live longer, healthier lives and enjoy a better quality of life in their golden years.

Avoiding Common Feeding Mistakes

While we have come to realize the benefits of proper dog nutrition, it is also important to be aware of common mistakes dog owners make. Let's look at them together:

- **The One-Size-Fits-All Diet:** Every dog is different, with varying nutritional needs based on characteristics such as age, breed, activity level, and health. Avoid using the same commercial diet for all dogs, and work with your veterinarian to find the optimal nutrition plan for your dog.

- **Overfeeding or Underfeeding:** Portion control is essential. Overeating can lead to obesity and other health problems, while underfeeding can lead to malnutrition and stunted growth.

- **Ignoring Ingredient Labels:** Always read dog food ingredient labels carefully. Look for high-quality ingredients and steer clear of those that are high in artificial ingredients or byproducts.

- **Inadequate Hydration:** Make sure your dog has access to clean, fresh water at all times. Dehydration can lead to a number of health problems.

- **Diet Inconsistency:** Frequently changing your dog's diet can disrupt their digestive system. Unless otherwise directed by your veterinarian, maintain a consistent diet with a regular brand.

Choosing the Best Dog Food

With so many choices, selecting the right dog food can be a challenging endeavor. Here are some tips to help you make an informed decision:

- **Consult a Veterinarian:** To determine your dog's exact nutritional needs, consult your veterinarian. They can suggest a diet based on your dog's age, breed, and overall health.

- **Check the Labels:** Look at the ingredient list. Seek out key ingredients, such as whole meats like chicken, beef, or fish. Avoid foods that contain a lot of additives and chemical preservatives.

- **Consider Your Dog's Age:** Newborn, adult, and senior dogs have different nutritional needs. Choose a food that is appropriate for your dog's stage of life.

- **Consider Special Needs:** If your dog has any special health concerns, such as allergies or sensitivities, consult your veterinarian to determine an appropriate diet.

- **Research Good Brands:** Not all dog food brands are equal. Choose reliable products that are known for their safety and quality.

- **Watch Your Dog's Reaction:** When introducing a new food, watch for any negative reactions or changes in behavior or well-being. This will help you determine if the food is a good fit.

The Influence of Diet on Canine Health

Now that we've covered the basics of canine nutrition, let's take a closer look at how proper nutrition affects the health and well-being of dogs.

1. **Weight Control**
   Studies have linked obesity in dogs to a number of health issues, including diabetes, osteoarthritis, and heart disease [13]. Maintaining an ideal weight requires proper nutrition and portion control.

2. **Dental Care**
   Dental health is primarily dependent on the type of food consumed. Feeding your dog dry food or oral chews to prevent tartar and plaque buildup can help maintain better teeth and gums [14].

3. **Skin and Coat Care**
   A beautiful, healthy coat is often a sign of proper nutrition. Particularly, studies have shown that Omega-3 fatty acids improve skin and coat health by reducing irritation and flaking [15].

4. **Digestive Wellness**
   Fibrous foods can help support gastrointestinal health by reducing constipation and diarrhea. In addition, probiotics and prebiotics can help maintain a healthy gut microbiota [16]. Probiotics are live microorganisms that, when administered in adequate amounts, confer health benefits on the host. In the context of canine nutrition, they help maintain the balance of the dog's intestinal flora, promoting healthy digestion.

5. **Joint Care**
   Diets with added Glucosamine and Chondroitin can improve joint health and reduce the risk of osteoarthritis in larger breeds or dogs prone to joint problems [17].

An Owner's Perspective

Making their own food for their dogs gives owners a greater sense of involvement in taking care of their pets [18]. Some pet owners want to be actively engaged in all aspects of their pet's care, including meal preparation.

Whether justified or not, a growing number of pet owners have questioned or believed the pre-prepared pet food supply to be unsafe [19]. For example, avoiding preservatives and grains in commercial diets is believed to improve their condition. Others seek a more appetizing, pure, and natural food for their dog, whose appetite has diminished, to help with their care.

Whatever the reason, dog owners who want to prepare food for their dogs at home find that the information they get from the Internet and books is inadequate and limited, yet they rarely visit the veterinarian. Dog owners frequently show interest in homemade diets for various reasons, such as [20]:

1. **Health Concerns:** Due to contaminants, preservatives, and additives.

2. **Label Confusion:** The inability to comprehend the labels on food packages, which provide information about the food item, the serving amount, and any associated uncertainty.

3. **Specific Medical Conditions:** Dogs with specific medical conditions such as chronic kidney disease, heart disease, and cancer often lack appropriate commercial products.

Because of these factors, it is important to provide dogs with a well-balanced homemade meal when the pet owner chooses to cook for them, and this book will fulfill all of your basic as well as advanced needs regarding cooking at home for your beloved dogs. When recommending natural foods, it's important to clarify that you cannot create a proper natural diet using hearsay and unsupported online articles [20]. Resources to meet this requirement should be based on scientific literature. It is possible to create a homemade diet for a healthy animal based on the dog's consumption rate and physiological condition.

Along with the diet, it is easy to alter the amount of nutrients, such as protein, fiber, and carbohydrates, to adapt to changing health conditions as the dog ages. In addition, homemade diets can be quite successful for dogs with food allergies. A veterinary nutritionist can guide you in diagnosing a food allergy or intolerance at home by separately testing one or two specific ingredients. As the allergic condition improves, you can introduce appropriate supplements one at a time to maintain the nutritional balance of the diet. Veterinarians and pet owners often prefer home cooking for the following reasons:

- **Individualized Nutrition:** Every dog is different, with specific nutritional needs that may change with age, breed, size, activity level, and underlying medical conditions. Home cooking allows pet owners to customize their dog's diet. Unlike commercial dog foods, which often have a "one size fits all" philosophy, homemade meals can tailor to provide the ideal ratio of proteins, carbohydrates, fats, vitamins, and minerals for each dog [21].

- **Quality Assurance:** Pet owners' main concern is the quality of the ingredients in their dog's food is one of the main concerns of pet owners. They have complete control over the source and selection of products when they prepare meals at home. As a result, they can choose premium, local, and fresh products to provide their dog with the best possible nutrition, free from questionable additives or preservatives [22]. Home-cooked meals, prepared and stored with care for cleanliness and freshness, encompass food safety as part of quality control.

- **Beneficial Ingredients:** Increased knowledge about the value of whole, natural foods has changed how we feed our dogs. Commercial dog foods commonly contain fillers, artificial flavors, and by-products, which may not be beneficial for your dog's health. When you cook at home, you can use natural products that provide essential nutrients without adding extraneous ingredients. This can help your pet to have better digestion, healthier skin and hair, and more stamina [23].

- **Allergen Management:** Dogs, like people, are susceptible to allergies or sensitivities to certain chemicals. When you prepare meals at home, it may be easier to identify and manage these allergies. Eliminate likely allergy triggers from your dog's food, such as grains, certain proteins, or artificial ingredients, and monitor the ingredients for any positive health improvements [24].

- **Weight Control:** Obesity in dogs is an evolving problem that can lead to several health issues [24]. Cooking at home can help you control your dog's weight more effectively. You can portion meals based on their caloric needs to make sure they get enough to maintain a healthy weight. Providing fresh, balanced meals helps keep your dog in shape [25].

- **Care and Bonding:** In addition to nutrition, feeding your dog at home also focuses on your relationship. Preparing food for your pet builds a closer bond and demonstrates your concern for their well-being. Each portion of food you prepare for your dog shows how much love you put into it, making mealtime a special time of connection [26].

- **Understanding the Nutritional Facts:** Many pet owners find that cooking at home helps them better understand their dog's nutritional needs. They become increasingly concerned about their pet's well-being as they research, learn about appropriate foods, and develop dietary concerns. This empowerment can lead to better long-term health outcomes [27]. Of course, it takes time and effort to study this subject.

Switching to Homemade Meals

It's important to remember that transitioning your dog to a home-cooked meal should be done gradually and under professional supervision. To ensure that your dog's dietary needs are met, consultation with a veterinarian or veterinary nutritionist is strongly recommended. Veterinarians can help you prepare balanced meals that meet your dog's nutritional needs and monitor your dog's health as they adapt to the new diet.

Focus On

For vets and pet owners, home cooking for dogs has become the preferred option. This is due to their ability to provide a personalized diet, quality control, superior ingredients, allergy prevention, weight management, and a closer bond with their canine companions.

This homemade, healthy dog food guide allows you to take charge of your dog's diet at a time when society is increasingly acknowledging the need to provide the best possible care for our pets. This strategy demonstrates a desire to provide the highest quality care, which ultimately enriches the lives of our beloved pets. The time and effort you put into cooking fresh meals for your dog will pay off in health and happiness, and the process will be fun for both you and your pet.

Use this guide to embark on a culinary adventure that will have your dog appreciating the food you prepare and wagging their tail in delight.

References

1. Udell, M.A. and C.D. Wynne, A review of domestic dogs'(Canis familiaris) human-like behaviors: or why behavior analysts should stop worrying and love their dogs. Journal of the experimental analysis of behavior, 2008. 89(2): p. 247-261.

2. Miklösi, Á., et al., Use of experimenter-given cues in dogs. Animal cognition, 1998. 1: p. 113-121.

3. Pitcairn, R.H. and S.H. Pitcairn, Dr. Pitcairn's complete guide to natural health for dogs & cats. 2017: Rodale.

4. Connolly, K.M., C.R. Heinze, and L.M. Freeman, Feeding practices of dog breeders in the United States and Canada. Journal of the American Veterinary Medical Association, 2014. 245(6): p. 669-676.

5. Hewson-Hughes, A.K., et al., Geometric analysis of macronutrient selection in the adult domestic cat, Felis catus. Journal of Experimental Biology, 2011. 214(6): p. 1039-1051.

6. Holscher, H.D., Dietary fiber and prebiotics and the gastrointestinal microbiota. Gut microbes, 2017. 8(2): p. 172-184.

7. Beynen, A.C., Fat content in dog food. Creature Companion, 2017: p. 40-41.

8. Council, N.R., Nutrient requirements of dogs and cats. 2006: National Academies Press.

9. Kim, H.-t., et al., Evaluation of selected ultra-trace minerals in commercially available dry dog foods. Veterinary Medicine: Research and Reports, 2018: p. 43-51.

10. Forrest, R., et al., The diets of companion cats in Aotearoa New Zealand: Identification of obesity risk factors. Animals, 2021. 11(10): p. 2881.

11. Oberbauer, A., et al., Ten inherited disorders in purebred dogs by functional breed groupings. Canine genetics and epidemiology, 2015. 2(1): p. 1-12.

12. Pedrinelli, V., et al., Predictive equations of maintenance energy requirement for healthy and chronically ill adult dogs. Journal of Animal Physiology and Animal Nutrition, 2021. 105: p. 63-69.

13. German, A.J., et al., Obesity, its associated disorders and the role of inflammatory adipokines in companion animals. The Veterinary Journal, 2010. 185(1): p. 4-9.

14. Bellows, J., et al., 2019 AAHA dental care guidelines for dogs and cats. Journal of the American Animal Hospital Association, 2019. 55(2): p. 49-69.

15. Marchegiani, A., et al., Impact of nutritional supplementation on canine dermatological disorders. Veterinary Sciences, 2020. 7(2): p. 38.

16. Jensen, A.P. and C.R. Bjørnvad, Clinical effect of probiotics in prevention or treatment of gastrointestinal disease in dogs: A systematic review. Journal of veterinary internal medicine, 2019. 33(5): p. 1849-1864.

17. Zhang, Z., et al., Curcumin slows osteoarthritis progression and relieves osteoarthritisassociated pain symptoms in a post-traumatic osteoarthritis mouse model. Arthritis research & therapy, 2016. 18(1): p. 1-12.

18. Remillard, R.L., Homemade diets: attributes, pitfalls, and a call for action. Topics in companion animal medicine, 2008. 23(3): p. 137-142.

19. Wakefield, L.A., F.S. Shofer, and K.E. Michel, Evaluation of cats fed vegetarian diets and attitudes of their caregivers. Journal of the American Veterinary Medical Association, 2006. 229(1): p. 70-73.

20. İnal, F., et al., P24-Köpekler İçin Doğal ve Dengeli Yemek Tariflerinin Test Edilmesi. 2022.

21. Dodds, W.J. and D. Laverdure, Canine nutrigenomics: the new science of feeding your dog for optimum health. 2014: Dogwise Publishing.

22. Kinnison, T. and R. Lumbis, Developing an interprofessional nutrition programme: Communication, in An Interprofessional Approach to Veterinary Nutrition. 2023, CABI GB. p. 71-94.

23. Wilson, S.A., et al., Evaluation of the nutritional adequacy of recipes for home-prepared maintenance diets for cats. Journal of the American Veterinary Medical Association, 2019. 254(10): p. 1172-1179.

24. Preet, G.S., et al., Dog obesity: Epidemiology, risk factors, diagnosis and management: A review paper. J. Pharm. Innov, 2021. 10: p. 698-705.

25. Gagne, J.W. and J.J. Wakshlag, Pathophysiology and clinical approach to malnutrition in dogs and cats. Nutritional management of hospitalized small animals, 2015: p. 117- 127.

26. Deldalle, S. and F. Gaunet, Effects of 2 training methods on stress-related behaviors of the dog (Canis familiaris) and on the dog–owner relationship. Journal of Veterinary Behavior, 2014. 9(2): p. 58-65.

27. Laflamme, D., Nutritional care for aging cats and dogs. Veterinary Clinics: Small Animal Practice, 2012. 42(4): p. 769-791.

PART 1. Toxic Ingredients in Dog Food: Exposing the Hidden Dangers

We, as responsible pet parents, strive to provide the best care and nutrition for our pets. But there are unseen dangers in our kitchens and pantries—dangerous food additives that can be harmful, even deadly, to our beloved pets.

We will delve deeper into the realm of toxic food ingredients for dogs in this thorough guide, highlighting the dangers, sharing real-life stories, and suggesting alternatives to keep our canine companions safe and healthy.

Understanding the Canine Digestive System

As we delve into the details of toxic food components, it's important to understand the dog's digestive tract. Dogs, unlike humans, possess a smaller and more acidic digestive system that facilitates the rapid digestion of animal-based lipids and proteins.

While this helps them thrive on a meat-based diet, it also makes them more susceptible to some dangerous compounds found in the human diet.

Let's take a closer look at some of these dangerous elements.

Toxic Ingredients in Dog Food

Let's now examine some specific toxic ingredients commonly found in our kitchens that can pose a risk to our pets, some of them are really dangerous.

But let's go in order:

1. **Chocolate: A Delicious Poison**
   Chocolate is a delicious treat for humans, but it can be deadly for dogs [1]. It contains Theobromine and Caffeine, which are stimulants that affect a dog's central nervous system and heart muscle. Bitter chocolate and cocoa powder contain the most Theobromine, making them the most dangerous.

2. **The Silent Killer: Xylitol**
   Xylitol, a sugar substitute used in sugar-free gum, candy, and baked goods, is extremely toxic to dogs. Even small doses can cause a rapid release of insulin, resulting in a serious drop in blood sugar (Hypoglycemia) and, in extreme cases, liver failure [2].

3. **Grapes and Raisins: A Dangerous Component**
   Contrary to popular belief, grapes and raisins are harmful to dogs. The specific component that causes their toxicity is unknown, although ingestion can cause kidney failure in certain dogs [3]. The degree of reaction varies among dogs.

4. **Onions and Garlic: Flavor Hazards**
   Onions and garlic, commonly found in many savory foods, contain thiosulfates, which can damage a dog's red blood cells and cause Hemolytic Anemia [4]. Signs may not show up right away, but they can develop over time.

5. **Dogs Should Avoid Alcohol**
   Dogs should not consume alcohol in any form, including beer, wine, or spirits [5]. Their systems lack the enzymes needed to digest alcohol, which makes it very dangerous and can cause intoxication, leading to serious health problems.

6. **Bones: A Dangerous Chew**
   Although many people provide bones for their dogs to chew on, it is important to take precautions [6]. Barbecued bones, especially chicken and turkey bones, may become brittle and shatter, causing internal injuries or obstructions in the dog's gastrointestinal tract. Instead, use specially formulated dog chews.

7. **Artificial Sweeteners Other than Xylitol**
   Xylitol is not the only artificial sweetener to avoid. Sorbitol, mannitol, and maltitol are other sugar-free ingredients that may be harmful to dogs [7]. It is important to check labels carefully.

8. **Avocado: A Dangerous Fruit**
   Avocado is a popular fruit for its healthy fats and minerals, but it also contains persin [8], which can be toxic to dogs in large amounts. Although you can usually tolerate modest amounts of avocado flesh, you should always remove the pit and skin.

9. **BHA and BHT: Artificial Ingredients of Concern**
   Butylated Hydroxyanisole (BHA) and Butylated Hydroxytoluene (BHT) are two synthetic antioxidants that are widely used in pet foods. Research suggests that they may be carcinogenic and should be avoided whenever possible [9]. Always read labels carefully.

10. **Synthetic Dyes**
    Studies have linked artificial food colorings to hyperactivity and allergic reactions in dogs. Choose natural alternatives or foods without added color [10].

Safe Alternatives and Treatments

Now that we've discussed the risks, it's important to understand what safe alternatives and foods you can give your pet. There are several options:

1. **Safe Fruits and Vegetables**
   Safe fruits and vegetables for dogs include apples, green beans, blueberries, and carrots in moderation [11]. Carefully remove all seeds, cores, and pits from the fruit and cut it into bite-sized pieces before giving it to your dog.

2. **Promotional Dog Treats**
   Brand-name dog treats that are high quality and vet-approved are designed to meet your dog's nutritional needs while tasting delicious [12]. Always look for treats made from natural ingredients.

3. **Customized Treats**
   You can make customized dog treats using dog-friendly foods like plain yogurt and oats [13]. You can tailor several online recipes to your dog's interests and nutritional needs.

4. **Dental Gums and Toys**
   Dental gums and toys not only entertain, but they also help to maintain your dog's dental hygiene. It is crucial to only buy products that have received approval from veterinary organizations.

Let us study two real-life examples to demonstrate the dangers of feeding these toxic chemicals to dogs.

Case Study 1: Max's Grape Misadventure

Over time, a Labrador Retriever by the name of Max developed a pattern of stealing food from the kitchen counter. One day, he was successful in grasping a large quantity of grapes. Up until the point that Max got lethargic and stopped eating, his owner was completely unconcerned. A visit to the veterinarian revealed that Max was suffering from grape poisoning, and his kidneys were weakening due to the condition. The path to recovery for Max was a long and uncertain one, and it required him to undergo intense care and adhere to a restricted diet.

Case Study 2: Bella's Xylitol Battle

While out for a stroll, Bella, a lively Pomeranian, and her owner stumbled upon an abandoned bag of tasty bubblegum. However, her owner was not aware that the gum contained Xylitol as an ingredient. Within hours of consuming it, Bella began to experience Hypoglycemia symptoms such as lethargy, nausea, and seizures associated with low blood sugar. The veterinarian rushed her, administered glucose, and closely monitored her condition throughout the entire process. It was possible to save Bella, but her owner was able to gain valuable knowledge about the risks associated with Xylitol.

These incidents are a stark warning that very common and seemingly harmless chemicals can have devastating effects on our pets. To prevent such accidents, it is important to be aware of harmful dietary ingredients.

Focus On

Dogs are beloved members of our family, and their safety and health must always come first. It is critical to understand the harmful food components that may affect them in order to provide the best care possible. Chocolate, alcohol, grapes, Xylitol, onions, artificial sweeteners, bones, and even seemingly healthy foods like avocado can all be harmful to our canine companions.

We can help our pets live happy, healthy lives by being aware of these dangers and avoiding unintentional toxicity. Instead of sharing potentially dangerous human food, offer appropriate alternatives and dog-specific treats. Let us keep our four-legged friends safe and keep their tails wagging for years to come.

References

1. Reddy, B.S. and L.V. Reddy, Sivajothi. Chocolate Poisoning in a Dog. Int J Vet Health Sci Res, 2013. 1(03): p. 16-17.

2. Schmid, R.D. and L.R. Hovda, Acute hepatic failure in a dog after xylitol ingestion. Journal of Medical Toxicology, 2016. 12(2): p. 201-205.

3. Wegenast, C.A., et al., Acute kidney injury in dogs following ingestion of cream of tartar and tamarinds and the connection to tartaric acid as the proposed toxic principle in grapes and raisins. Journal of Veterinary Emergency and Critical Care, 2022. 32(6): p. 812-816.

4. Salgado, B., L. Monteiro, and N.S. Rocha, Allium species poisoning in dogs and cats. Journal of Venomous Animals and Toxins including Tropical Diseases, 2011. 17: p. 4- 11.

5. Van Wuijckhuise, L. and G. Cremers, Alcohol poisoning in dogs. Tijdschrift voor Diergeneeskunde, 2003. 128(9): p. 284-285.

6. Cohen, H.-Y., The risk of bones. Veterinary Nursing Journal, 2006. 21(12): p. 21-22.

7. Larsen, J.C., Artificial sweeteners: A brief review of their safety issues. Nutrafoods, 2012. 11: p. 3-9.

8. Davenport, G.M., et al., Tolerance and safety of an avocado-based ingredient for adult dogs. 2012, Wiley Online Library. https://doi.org/10.1096/fasebj.26.1_supplement.825.1

9. Costa, J., et al., Concentration of synthetic antioxidants and peroxide value of commercial dry pet foods. Animal Feed Science and Technology, 2022: p. 115499.

10. Hofve, J., Is Food Coloring Safe For Dogs? 2022.

11. ALIVE, P.H., Fruits and Vegetables Safe for Dogs. 2022, Obtenido de https://www. homesalive. ca/blog/fruits-vegetables-fordogs.

12. Yankowicz, S., What ingredients to look for in dog food and treats. TRVP Guide, 2022.

13. Liou, W., Divine Dog Treats: Recipes for a Happy, Healthy Pet. 2010: iUniverse.

PART 2. Feeding for Dogs with Special Needs: Obesity, Diabetes, Old Age, and Renal Diseases

Obesity, Diabetes, and kidney disease are some of the health problems that our dogs can face as they get older, but they can also affect young dogs.

Proper nutrition is essential to controlling and preventing these conditions, as well as protecting the overall health of our beloved dogs. Nutrition has the ability to directly modify disease states by providing substances such as macro- and micronutrients, as well as indirectly by influencing the gut microbiota, which in turn influences the response to nutrition.

Now that we've acknowledged the broader health challenges such as obesity, diabetes, and kidney disease, let's dive deeper into the dietary management of each condition [1].

In this in-depth chapter, we will look at the factual elements of nutritional treatment for obese dogs, diabetic dogs, geriatric dogs, and dogs with kidney problems, based on the latest research and expert suggestions.

Each section will include information on specific nutritional issues based on scientific references, as well as practical suggestions for maintaining proper nutritional care.

Managing an Overweight Dog's Diet

In general, pet obesity is a significant problem, and canine obesity is a growing concern. According to a recent report from the Association for Pet Obesity Prevention, 56% of dogs in the United States are considered overweight or obese [2].

Obesity is also associated with a number of other diseases, including diabetes, osteoarthritis, and cardiovascular disease, just as in humans [3]. As a result, it is critical to address this condition with proper nutrition. Let's see how:

1. **Weight Control with Calorie Restriction**
   Caloric restriction is one of the most common techniques used to treat obesity in dogs. It involves reducing the dog's daily caloric intake, often by feeding a calorie-controlled diet. A study conducted by Linder and Freeman [4] found that caloric restriction can significantly improve the lives of dogs and reduce obesity.

2. **Protein Content**
   Reducing calories is important for weight loss, but so is getting enough protein. Protein helps to maintain lean muscle mass during weight loss. German and Holden [5] found that a balanced, high-quality protein diet is important for obese dogs.

3. **High-Fiber Diets**
   Obese dogs often receive high-fiber diet recommendations as they can feel fuller while consuming fewer calories. Dietary fiber, while not providing calories, plays a crucial role in weight management by helping to increase satiety and reducing overall caloric intake. Peña and Suarez [6] found that high-fiber diets can actually help dogs lose weight.

Managing the Diabetic Dog's Diet

Here is an overview of diabetes in dogs. Diabetes mellitus (DM) is becoming increasingly common in cats and dogs, with the incidence of diabetes in dogs increasing by 79.7% [7].

Diabetes, defined by a decrease in the synthesis or action of insulin, is a major health problem in dogs. DM in dogs is managed by stabilizing blood glucose levels with proper nutrition.

Let's be a little more specific:

1. **High-Quality Protein**
   Maintaining a healthy protein intake is critical for diabetic dogs, just as it is for humans. High-quality protein can help with blood glucose regulation. Blood glucose regulation involves maintaining stable blood sugar levels, which is essential for preventing the spikes and drops that can be harmful, especially in diabetic dogs. Elliott and Rand [8] emphasized the importance of protein quality in managing canine diabetes.

2. **Carbohydrate Management**
   Limiting carbohydrate intake is critical in the management of canine diabetes [8]. We prefer low-glycemic-index (GI) carbohydrates as they lead to lower and more consistent blood glucose levels. The glycemic index measures how foods impact blood glucose levels. Low GI foods absorb more slowly, leading to a more gradual rise in blood sugar levels. Bennett and Greco [9] conducted a study showing the benefits of a restricted diet for diabetic dogs.

3. **Consistent Feeding Schedule**
   A consistent feeding schedule for diabetic dogs helps with insulin therapy and blood glucose regulation. This stability improves disease control and minimizes blood glucose fluctuations [10].

Nutritional Needs of Senior Dogs

We will now learn how to meet the special needs of older dogs. The nutritional needs of dogs change as they age. Senior dogs often require diets that promote joint mobility, brain function, and overall vitality [11]. Scientific research has provided valuable insight into meeting these needs.

With a clear understanding of the general changes in dietary needs as dogs age, let's now examine the specific nutrients and supplements that can significantly enhance their quality of life.

1. **Joint Support Supplements**
   Older dogs are more susceptible to joint problems, such as osteoarthritis. Studies have demonstrated that Glucosamine and Chondroitin sulfate supplements enhance the joint health of older dogs. These substances are natural compounds found in cartilage that help rebuild cartilage and lubricate joints, making them crucial for managing arthritis and other joint issues. According to research by Bhathal and Spryszak [12], these supplements help increase mobility and reduce discomfort.

2. **Cognitive Support**
   Mental impairment in older dogs, similar to dementia in humans, is possible. Studies have linked certain foods, such as antioxidants, Omega-3 fatty acids, and vitamins E and C, to cognitive support. Nutrients like these are essential for maintaining neural health, particularly in preventing or slowing the progression of cognitive decline in senior dogs. Landsberg and Araujo [13] investigated the role of these substances in maintaining cognitive function in older dogs.

3. **Reduced Caloric Intake**
   Older dogs have reduced energy requirements, so maintaining an appropriate caloric intake can help prevent obesity in senior dogs. Adjusting portion sizes and using foods designed for older dogs can alleviate this problem [14].

Nutritional Support for a Dog with Kidney Disease

Renal (kidney) problems, particularly chronic kidney disease (CKD), are common in senior dogs [15]. Proper nutrition is critical to helping dogs with kidney disease. Having outlined the challenges CKD poses for our canine companions, let's explore the specific dietary modifications that can help mitigate these issues and support kidney function.

1. **Diets Low in Phosphorus**
   Studies such as Polzin's [16] have shown that reducing phosphorus intake can slow the progression of CKD in dogs. Therefore, doctors often prescribe special low-phosphorus diets for dogs with kidney problems. We specifically formulate these diets to reduce the amount of phosphorus dogs ingest, a crucial step given the link between high phosphorus consumption and worsening kidney function in dogs with CKD.

2. **Reducing Dietary Protein (When Necessary)**
   A low protein diet may be beneficial for some dogs with kidney disease. Reduced protein levels may reduce stress on the kidneys. However, it is important to consult with a veterinarian, as not all dogs with kidney problems need to limit their protein intake [17].

3. **Omega-3 Fatty Acids**
   Anti-inflammatory Omega-3 fatty acids, such as those found in fish oil, may help dogs with kidney problems [18]. According to Brown and Elliott [19], Omega-3 therapy may help treat inflammation associated with CKD. The body cannot produce Omega-3 fatty acids, necessitating their acquisition from food. They are known for their anti-inflammatory properties and play a crucial role in maintaining kidney health in dogs with CKD.

Focus On

A healthy, balanced diet is a critical component of care for obese, diabetic, geriatric, and kidney disease dogs. Scientific evidence supports the use of specific dietary approaches to manage and prevent chronic diseases, as well as improve the quality of life and lifespan of our beloved canine friends.

A balanced diet tailored to their specific needs can have a significant impact on their health and well-being. Visit your veterinarian to develop a customized nutrition plan for your pet's specific health conditions and needs.

References

1. Suez, J. and E. Elinav, The path towards microbiome-based metabolite treatment. Nature microbiology, 2017. 2(6): p. 1-5.

2. Prevention, A.f.P.O., U.S. Pet Obesity Rates Plateau and Nutritional Confusion Grows. 2019.

3. Phillips, A.M., et al., Feline obesity in veterinary medicine: insights from a thematic analysis of communication in practice. Frontiers in Veterinary Science, 2017. 4: p. 117.

4. Linder, D.E., et al., Status of selected nutrients in obese dogs undergoing caloric restriction. BMC veterinary research, 2013. 9: p. 1-10.

5. German, A.J., et al., A high protein high fiber diet improves weight loss in obese dogs. The Veterinary Journal, 2010. 183(3): p. 294-297.

6. Peña, C., et al., Effects of low-fat high-fiber diet and mitratapide on body weight reduction, blood pressure and metabolic parameters in obese dogs. Journal of Veterinary Medical Science, 2014. 76(9): p. 1305-1308.

7. Hospital, B.A., State of Pet Health§ 2016 Report. 2016.

8. Elliott, K., et al., A diet lower in digestible carbohydrate results in lower postprandial glucose concentrations compared with a traditional canine diabetes diet and an adult maintenance diet in healthy dogs. Research in veterinary science, 2012. 93(1): p. 288- 295.

9. Bennett, N., et al., Comparison of a low carbohydrate–low fiber diet and a moderate carbohydrate–high fiber diet in the management of feline diabetes mellitus. Journal of feline medicine and surgery, 2006. 8(2): p. 73-84.

10. Rucinsky, R., et al., AAHA diabetes management guidelines for dogs and cats. Journal of the American Animal Hospital Association, 2010. 46(3): p. 215-224.

11. Hutchinson, D., et al., Survey of Opinions About Nutritional Requirements of Senior Dogs and Analysis of Nutrient Profiles of Commercially Available Diets for Senior Dogs. International Journal of Applied Research in Veterinary Medicine, 2011. 9(1).

12. Bhathal, A., et al., Glucosamine and Chondroitin use in canines for osteoarthritis: A review. Open veterinary journal, 2017. 7(1): p. 36-49.

13. Landsberg, G. and J.A. Araujo, Behavior problems in geriatric pets. Veterinary Clinics: Small Animal Practice, 2005. 35(3): p. 675-698.

14. Vendramini, T.H.A., et al., Profile qualitative variables on the dynamics of weight loss programs

in dogs. Plos one, 2022. 17(1): p. e0261946.

15. Bartges, J.W., Chronic kidney disease in dogs and cats. Veterinary Clinics: Small Animal Practice, 2012. 42(4): p. 669-692.

16. Polzin, D.J., Chronic kidney disease in small animals. Veterinary Clinics: Small Animal Practice, 2011. 41(1): p. 15-30.

17. Böswald, L., E. Kienzle, and B. Dobenecker, Observation about phosphorus and protein supply in cats and dogs prior to the diagnosis of chronic kidney disease. Journal of animal physiology and animal nutrition, 2018. 102: p. 31-36.

18. Bauer, J.E., The essential nature of dietary Omega-3 Fatty Acids in dogs. Journal of the American Veterinary Medical Association, 2016. 249(11): p. 1267-1272.

19. Brown, C., et al., Chronic kidney disease in aged cats: clinical features, morphology, and proposed pathogeneses. Veterinary pathology, 2016. 53(2): p. 309-326.

PART 3. Feeding Dogs with Chronic Conditions: Osteoarthritis, Cancer, Skin and Coat Problems, Cardiovascular and Heart Disease

Nutritional management is critical to maintaining the overall health and well-being of dogs [1]. Various diseases, just as in humans, require individualized nutritional strategies to control symptoms, support therapy, and improve the quality of life for our furry friends.

This section provides a comprehensive understanding of nutritional requirements, treatment options, and management strategies for various diseases.

In this complete guide, we will explore the importance of nutrition for dogs with osteoarthritis, cancer, skin and coat problems, and cardiovascular and heart disease.

Each section will include information on specific nutritional issues based on scientific references, as well as practical suggestions for maintaining proper nutritional care.

Canine Osteoarthritis Nutritional Management

Particularly common in older dogs, osteoarthritis is an inflammation of the joints that causes pain and limited mobility. Osteoarthritis (OA) is a degenerative joint disease in dogs characterized by the gradual degeneration of the articular structures and subchondral tissue. It often causes discomfort, stiffness, and a decreased range of motion. OA is a common dog condition, with a prevalence of 2.5 percent in UK veterinary primary care clinics [2]. OA can affect any joint, including the pelvis, knees, ankles, and hocks, as well as the facet joints of the spine, wrist, and tarsal joints [3].

Nutritional management is critical to maintaining the overall health and well-being of dogs. Various diseases, just as in humans, require individualized nutritional strategies to control symptoms, support therapy, and improve the quality of life for our furry friends. After understanding the general impact of nutrition on chronic conditions, let's delve into how specific dietary components can manage and alleviate osteoarthritis symptoms in dogs. Proper nutrition can significantly reduce OA symptoms and improve a dog's quality of life. Here's how:

1. **Joint Supporting Nutrients**

   ○ **Glucosamine and Chondroitin Sulfate:** These compounds are known to support joint health by promoting cartilage production and regeneration [4]. They are naturally occurring substances that help build and maintain cartilage, which is crucial for joint health and mobility. Various joint supplements and specially formulated joint foods for dogs contain them.

   ○ **Omega-3 Fatty Acids:** The anti-inflammatory properties of Omega-3 fatty acids, particularly EPA and DHA from sources such as fish oil, may help reduce joint damage and discomfort [5]. Eicosapentaenoic Acid (EPA) and Docosahexaenoic Acid (DHA) are types of Omega-3 fatty acids known for their strong anti-inflammatory properties, making them essential in diets aimed at reducing inflammation and supporting joint health.

   ○ **Antioxidants:** Studies have shown that vitamins C and E, along with other antioxidants, can reduce oxidative stress in the joints and prevent the progression of OA [6].

2. **Weight Control**
   Excess weight puts additional stress on the joints in dogs with OA, so maintaining an optimal body weight is critical [7]. Check with your veterinarian to determine the proper calorie and weight control diet for your dog.

3. **Prescriptions and Therapeutic Diets**
   Some prescription diets designed for joint health, such as Hill's Prescription Diet j/d, contain a balanced blend of nutrients that may help dogs with OA [8].

Note: *(Not to advertise, but to explain.)* Hill's Pet Nutrition, a subsidiary of the Colgate-Palmolive Company, produces the specialty line of pet food known as Hill's Prescription Diet j/d. The goal of this product is to promote joint health in both dogs and cats. The letter "j/d" in its name stands for "joint diet." To enhance joint health, we formulate the food with specific ingredients. These often include high levels of Omega-3 fatty acids, which are known to reduce inflammation, and Glucosamine and Chondroitin, which are common supplements used to support joint health.

Vets also formulate the food to provide an appropriate balance of other nutrients to support overall health. Vets typically recommend Hill's Prescription Diet j/d for pets with specific joint health needs. Veterinarians should supervise this diet, which is part of a range of "prescription" diets formulated for pets with a variety of health problems. This is due to the fact that these diets cater to specific health conditions, which may not make them suitable for all pets.

Again, I will never tire of saying this: It is important to work with a vet to develop a special diet plan to meet the unique needs of your dog with OA. Routine check-ups will allow you to monitor your dog's progress and adjust the diet as needed.

Nutritional Support for Canine Cancer

In dogs, the cancer incidence rate was 0.804 percent for malignant tumors and 0.897 percent for benign tumors annually [9]. Cancer is the leading cause of death in dogs, and nutritional care can help support cancer therapy, minimize side effects, and improve the general well-being of affected dogs.

Understanding the significant impact of cancer on our canine friends, let's explore specific nutritional strategies that can support them through their treatment and recovery.

1. **Quality Protein**
   Protein is necessary to maintain muscle mass, which is especially critical in dogs with cancer [10]. High-quality protein sources, such as lean meats, can help meet the body's nutritional needs. Quality protein refers to highly digestible, lean sources of protein that provide all the essential amino acids necessary to support bodily functions without excessive fat, which can be especially beneficial for maintaining muscle mass in cancer-affected dogs.

2. **Calorie Density**
   Depending on the type and stage of the tumor, dogs may require a higher-calorie diet to prevent muscle loss and provide energy [11]. High-calorie diets are available specifically for cancer patients.

3. **Omega-3 Fatty Acids**
   Cancer and its therapies may cause inflammation, which Omega-3 fatty acids can help reduce [12]. Include fish oil pills in your dog's diet to get these healthy fats. Omega-3 fatty acids, including EPA and DHA, are known for their anti-inflammatory properties, which can help mitigate inflammatory responses associated with cancer and its treatments, thereby potentially reducing discomfort and enhancing overall health.

4. **Digestibility**
   To reduce gastrointestinal upset, which is common in dogs with cancer, choose easily digestible foods [13].

Working closely with a veterinarian is essential when developing a nutritional plan for your dog's unique cancer diagnosis. They can suggest appropriate dietary changes and supplements.

Nutrition for Canine Skin and Coat Problems

A dog's skin and coat are indicators of their overall health [14]. Itching, dryness, redness, and hair loss are all symptoms of skin problems.

Now that we understand the significance of skin and coat health as reflections of overall well-being, let's look at the specific nutrients that can help alleviate these common skin issues.

1. **Essential Fatty Acids**
   Skin health requires omega-6 and omega-3 fatty acids [15]. They help maintain skin hydration, reduce irritation, and promote a shiny coat. Essential fatty acids, particularly omega-6 and omega-3, are crucial for maintaining the skin's lipid barrier, which helps retain moisture and protect against environmental irritants. Use fish oil supplements or dog foods high in fatty acids.

2. **Protein Quality**
   Proteins are the building blocks of healthy skin and hair [16]. High-quality protein provides the amino acids necessary for the repair and regeneration of skin cells and hair follicles, supporting both the structure and function of the skin. Make sure your dog's food contains protein-rich sources such as meat, chicken, or seafood.

3. **Food Allergies**
   Food allergies may cause skin problems [17]. Consult your veterinarian to identify and treat any allergies in your dog's food.

4. **Hydration**
   Adequate hydration is essential for maintaining the skin's elasticity and suppleness, as well as preventing scales and excessive dryness. Always provide clean, fresh water for your dog.

If your dog has recurring skin and coat abnormalities, see a veterinarian to rule out parasites, fungal infections, or underlying health problems, as well as for advice on dietary changes.

Canine Cardiovascular and Heart Disease Nutritional Needs

Heart disease, such as congestive heart failure (CHF), is common in older dogs [18]. Dietary management can supplement medical management and improve cardiac function. Having established the critical role of nutrition in supporting cardiac health, let's delve into the specific dietary modifications that can help manage symptoms and improve the quality of life for dogs with heart disease.

1. **Sodium Restriction**
   Reducing sodium (salt) intake can help manage fluid accumulation in the chest and abdomen, a typical sign of CHF [19]. Sodium restriction in the diet helps manage fluid retention, a common issue in heart disease, by limiting the amount of salt that can cause water to accumulate in the body. Choose a low-sodium dog food or consult your veterinarian.

2. **L-Carnitine and Taurine**
   L-Carnitine and Taurine are two amino acids necessary for cardiovascular health [20]. A few breeds of dogs, such as Doberman Pinschers, are likely to develop heart disease due to Taurine deficiency. L-Carnitine and Taurine are vital for heart muscle function and energy production, and deficiencies in these amino acids are linked to certain types of heart diseases in dogs. Make sure your dog's food contains adequate amounts of these nutrients.

3. **Weight Management**
   In dogs with heart disease, excess weight can put stress on the heart, so maintaining a healthy body weight is critical [21]. Work with your veterinarian to develop a weight management strategy that is specific to your dog's needs.

4. **Antioxidants**
   Antioxidants such as vitamins C and E can help minimize the effects of oxidative stress on the heart [22]. Cardiac dog foods may incorporate them.

Always consult a veterinarian with experience treating heart problems for nutritional advice and to monitor your dog's progress.

Focus On

Proper nutritional management is critical to the health and well-being of dogs with different medical problems. Whether your pet has osteoarthritis, cancer, skin and coat problems, or cardiovascular and heart disease, a well-balanced diet can help support therapy, alleviate symptoms, and improve quality of life.

Consult a veterinarian to develop a diet plan tailored to your dog's individual needs, and keep in mind that frequent checkups and dietary adjustments may be necessary to maintain the best possible outcome for your furry friend.

References

1. Bontempo, V., Nutrition and health of dogs and cats: evolution of petfood. Veterinary research communications, 2005. 29: p. 45-50.

2. Anderson, K.L., et al., Prevalence, duration and risk factors for appendicular osteoarthritis in a UK dog population under primary veterinary care. Scientific reports, 2018. 8(1): p. 5641.

3. Franklin, S.P., R.D. Park, and E.L. Egger, Metacarpophalangeal and metatarsophalangeal osteoarthritis in 49 dogs. Journal of the American Animal Hospital Association, 2009. 45(3): p. 112-117.

4. Muzzarelli, R.A., et al., Chitosan, hyaluronan and chondroitin sulfate in tissue engineering for cartilage regeneration: a review. Carbohydrate polymers, 2012. 89(3): p. 723-739.

5. Zivkovic, A.M., et al., Dietary Omega-3 Fatty Acids aid in the modulation of inflammation and metabolic health. California agriculture, 2011. 65(3): p. 106.

6. Chin, K.-Y. and S. Ima-Nirwana, The role of vitamin E in preventing and treating osteoarthritis—a review of the current evidence. Frontiers in pharmacology, 2018. 9: p. 946.

7. Valverde, S. and C.M. Evason, Reduced activity/behavioral changes.

8. Budsberg, S.C. and J.W. Bartges, Nutrition and osteoarthritis in dogs: does it help? Veterinary Clinics: Small Animal Practice, 2006. 36(6): p. 1307-1323.

9. Baioni, E., et al., Estimating canine cancer incidence: findings from a population-based tumor registry in northwestern Italy. BMC veterinary research, 2017. 13(1): p. 1-9.

10. Case, L.P., et al., Canine and feline nutrition: a resource for companion animal professionals. 2010: Elsevier Health Sciences.

11. Cline, M.G., et al., 2021 AAHA nutrition and weight management guidelines for dogs and cats. Journal of the American Animal Hospital Association, 2021. 57(4): p. 153- 178.

12. Laviano, A., et al., Omega-3 Fatty Acids in cancer. Current Opinion in Clinical Nutrition & Metabolic Care, 2013. 16(2): p. 156-161.

13. Ogilvie, G.K., Nutrition and Cancer: Frontiers for Cure! Proceedings of the World Small Animal Veterinary Association, Prague, Czech Republic, 2006.

14. Hnilica, K.A. and A.P. Patterson, Small Animal Dermatology-E-Book: A Color Atlas and Therapeutic Guide. 2016: Elsevier Health Sciences.

15. Balić, A., et al., Omega-3 versus Omega-6 polyunsaturated fatty acids in the prevention and treatment of inflammatory skin diseases. International journal of molecular sciences, 2020. 21(3): p. 741.

16. Kumar, P., et al., Role of micro-nutrients in dermatological disorders of dog. Intas Polivet, 2007. 8(2): p. 467-471.

17. Hill, P., et al., Survey of the prevalence, diagnosis and treatment of dermatological conditions in small animals in general practice. Veterinary record, 2006. 158(16): p. 533-539.

18. Falk, T., et al., Arteriosclerotic changes in the myocardium, lung, and kidney in dogs with chronic congestive heart failure and myxomatous mitral valve disease. Cardiovascular Pathology, 2006. 15(4): p. 185-193.

19. Fuentes, V.L., Treatment of congestive heart failure, in BSAVA manual of canine and feline cardiorespiratory medicine. 2010, BSAVA Library. p. 153-159.

20. Sanderson, S.L., Taurine and Carnitine in canine cardiomyopathy. Veterinary Clinics: Small Animal Practice, 2006. 36(6): p. 1325-1343.

21. Morita, T., et al., The repeatability and characteristics of right ventricular longitudinal strain imaging by speckle-tracking echocardiography in healthy dogs. Journal of Veterinary Cardiology, 2017. 19(4): p. 351-362.

22. Van der Pol, A., et al., Treating oxidative stress in heart failure: past, present and future. European Journal of Heart Failure, 2019. 21(4): p. 425-435.

PART 4. Nutrition Management for Puppy, Weaned, Pregnant, and Lactating Dogs

We, as responsible dog owners, want to ensure that our canine friends receive the best possible care throughout their lives [1]. Nutrition is critical to a dog's health and well-being, especially during important life stages.

Puppies, pregnant dogs, and lactating mothers all have nutritional needs that are critical to their health and well-being [2]. Proper nutrition during these important life stages supports puppy development and growth, maintains pregnant dogs' well-being, and helps nursing mothers produce nutritious milk for their puppies.

In this section, we will look at the nutritional needs of puppies as well as the special needs of pregnant and nursing mothers. We will also discuss the process of weaning, which is the transition from puppy breast milk to regular food.

Puppy Nutritional Requirements

Now that we've highlighted the importance of nutrition during key life stages, let's focus specifically on the unique nutritional requirements of puppies, which lay the foundation for their future health and development. Puppies are energetic and inquisitive, and their nutritional needs differ from those of adult dogs [3]. You must feed them several times a day to meet their energy needs. Here are some important things to keep in mind when feeding puppies:

- **The Importance of Mother's Milk**
  Breast milk, also known as colostrum, contains important nutrients, antibodies, and growth regulators that aid in a puppy's development [4]. Colostrum strengthens the puppy's digestive tract and provides passive protection against disease. The first form of milk produced by the mother immediately following birth is rich in antibodies and essential nutrients, providing puppies with a critical boost in immunity and initial growth. This early nutrition is crucial because it helps prevent health problems later in life.

- **Premium Puppy Food**
  When selecting puppy food, opt for products specifically designed for them [5]. The formulation of these foods caters to the unique requirements of developing dogs. They have more proteins, lipids, vitamins, and minerals to support development and growth.

- **A Healthy Diet**
  Puppies need a balanced diet to ensure they get all the nutrients they need [6]. The Association of American Feed Control Officials (AAFCO) establishes minimum nutritional requirements for puppies, which manufacturers follow in developing their products. The AAFCO sets guidelines for nutritional adequacy in pet foods, ensuring that products meet specific standards suitable for various stages of a dog's life.

- **Adequate Nutrition**
  Adequate nutrition is essential throughout their growth period. Compared to adult dogs, puppies have smaller stomachs and higher caloric needs [7].

Puppy Feeding Schedule

1. **The Frequency of Meals**
   Depends on age [8]:

   - 6 to 12 weeks: four meals a day

   - 3 to 6 months: three meals a day

   - 6 to 12 months: two meals a day

2. **Protein**
   Puppies need a higher percentage of protein in their diet than adult dogs for muscle growth and cell formation [9]. Look for a puppy meal with 22–32 percent protein.

3. **Fat**
   Fat contains essential fatty acids and is an important source of energy. It is critical not only for energy, but also for proper brain function and nerve impulse transmission [10]. Puppies need a higher fat content in their diets than adult dogs. Choose foods with a fat content of 8 to 12 percent.

4. **Phosphorus and Calcium**
   Phosphorus and calcium are essential for bone growth [11]. To prevent skeletal problems, maintain a calcium-to-phosphorus ratio of 1:1 to 1.3:1. Avoid supplements unless a veterinarian prescribes them.

Transitional Diet

Puppies often begin eating solid foods at 3–4 weeks of age [12]. To facilitate this transition, mix wet or moist puppy food with milk replacer and their mother's milk.

It is important to choose a premium puppy food that meets their nutritional needs. Look for AAFCO (Association of American Feed Control Officials)-approved foods that are designed to provide adequate nutrition.

Weaning the Puppy

The practice of switching puppies from breast milk to regular food is known as weaning [13]. It is an important stage in a puppy's growth. Now that we understand what weaning entails, let's explore step-by-step methods to ensure a smooth and healthy transition from mother's milk to solid food.

- **Timing**
  Weaning typically begins at about 3–4 weeks of age, when puppies show interest in a normal diet [14]. You should complete it by 6-8 weeks of age.

- **Gradual Transition**
  To create a chunky soup texture, combine the puppy food with hot water or a puppy milk substitute [15]. This method is part of a gradual transition that involves slowly introducing solid food into the puppy's diet to allow their digestive systems to adjust without causing distress or nutritional imbalances. Encourage puppies to lick or swallow the mixture. Slowly reduce the amount of water and increase the amount of solid food.

- **Interaction with Others**
  Weaning is also an opportunity for puppies to develop social skills [16]. To promote socialization, encourage sibling contact during feeding. Social interaction during feeding not only helps puppies learn to eat solid food but also aids in their social development by interacting with siblings and humans.

- **Individualized Nutrition**
  As puppies become more adept at eating regular food, provide individual portions in separate bowls to ensure that each puppy gets its fair share and to track their progress [17]. Be careful, because there is always the most voracious puppy who will try to eat his little brothers' gruel in addition to his own.

- **Monitor Weight Gain**
  Weigh puppies regularly to confirm that they are gaining weight gradually [18]. Regular weighing ensures that each puppy is progressing healthily and helps in the early detection of any potential issues that might require veterinary attention. If you notice any weight loss or other health problems, contact your veterinarian.

Nutrition for the Pregnant Dog

Dog mothers have special nutritional needs to maintain their health and the growth of their offspring [19], so improved nutrition during pregnancy is essential. We divide this stage into three trimesters, each with specific nutritional needs [20]. With the fundamental importance of nutrition established, let's examine how a pregnant dog's dietary requirements evolve throughout each trimester.

- **First Trimester**
  A pregnant dog's energy needs remain fairly constant during the first trimester of pregnancy. However, we must feed her a high-quality diet that meets her maintenance energy needs. A high-quality diet for a pregnant dog includes balanced proportions of protein, fats, and carbohydrates, all sourced from highly digestible, premium ingredients to support overall health and fetal development.

- **Second Trimester**
  As the puppies grow during the second trimester of pregnancy, the mother dog's energy needs increase steadily. Any food provided should include appropriate protein, fat, and vitamins to support this growth.

- **Third Trimester**
  As puppies grow rapidly during the third trimester of pregnancy, the mother dog's energy needs continue to increase. Providing a meal specifically designed for pregnant dogs can help meet these additional needs while maintaining the health of both the mother and her developing puppies.

Important Considerations When Feeding a Pregnant Dog

- **Consult a Veterinarian**
  Talk to your veterinarian before making any dietary changes. Experts can recommend the best nutrition based on her breed, age, and the number of puppies she is carrying.

- **Gradually Increasing Calories**
  As her pregnancy progresses, a mother dog needs more calories [21]. This is especially true during the third trimester of pregnancy, when puppy development is most rapid.

- **Superior Dog Food**
  Switch to a higher-quality dog food designed specifically for pregnant dogs. Specifically formulated to meet the increased nutritional demands of gestation, premium dog food for pregnant dogs ensures the provision of essential nutrients in adequate amounts to support both the mother and the growing puppies.

- **Gradual Transition**
  To minimize stomach upset, introduce your pregnant dog to her new diet gradually. Begin early in the pregnancy.

- **Feed Regularly**
  Divide the daily caloric intake into many smaller portions to avoid distress to the pregnant dog's intestines and ensure that she gets the nutrients she needs each day [22].

- **Dietary Supplements**
  Under certain circumstances, your veterinarian may recommend certain supplements, such as calcium and folic acid. Excess nutrients can be dangerous if taken without competent advice.

The Nutritional Needs of the Feeding Dog

Lactating dogs, often referred to as "Nursing Moms," have increased nutritional needs to provide milk for their puppies. During this stage, good nutrition ensures the growth and health of the mother and her litter.

Recognizing the increased nutritional demands of nursing mothers, let's explore the specific dietary adjustments that can support them during this critical period.

- **Superior Dog Food**
  Throughout the lactation period, continue to feed superior-quality dog food designed for pregnant dogs. These foods' unique design encourages milk production. The formulation of superior dog food for lactating dogs supports high energy demands and includes enhanced levels of key nutrients like proteins and fats, which are crucial for milk production and maternal health.

- **Increase Calories**
  Lactating dogs need more energy than pregnant dogs to produce milk and for the mother's physical health. Monitor the mother's weight and make necessary adjustments to her calorie intake.

- **Adequate Hydration**
  Ensure that the nursing mother has a constant supply of fresh, clean water. Nursing can increase a dog's thirst for water. Adequate hydration is critical for lactating dogs because it directly affects milk volume and quality, ensuring that puppies receive the necessary hydration and nutrition from their mother's milk. Thirst can have an impact on milk production and the mother's well-being.

- **Monitor the Mother's Health**
  Routinely check the mother's condition, weight, and general health. Address any signs of nutritional imbalance or health problems as soon as possible.

- **Gradual Weaning**
  The mother's milk supply will usually decrease as the puppies begin to eat regular meals. Follow the puppies' development, and gradually reduce the mother's food intake as they become more dependent on regular food.

Focus On

Proper nutrition for puppies, weaning, and pregnant and lactating dogs is critical to the health and well-being of the mother and her puppies.

It is essential for good development, bone growth, and overall health that these dogs receive the optimal combination of nutrients at every stage of development, especially during critical periods such as puppyhood and pregnancy. Ask your veterinarian for individualized advice on your dog's nutritional needs, which may vary by breed, size, and overall health.

You can provide the best quality care for your furry friends by recognizing their nutritional needs, which are based on empirical research, and selecting high-quality, well-balanced foods. With the right nutrition, you can help your puppies grow into strong, healthy, and happy dogs, as well as help pregnant and lactating mothers raise their babies and enjoy a healthier and more joyful lifestyle.

References

1. Wood, L., et al., The pet factor-companion animals as a conduit for getting to know people, friendship formation and social support. PloS one, 2015. 10(4): p. e0122085.

2. McGinnis, T., The well dog book: The classic comprehensive handbook of dog care. 2014: Random House.

3. Hemmings, C., The importance of good nutrition in growing puppies and kittens. The Veterinary Nurse, 2016. 7(8): p. 450-456.

4. Rossi, L., et al., Nutritional and functional properties of colostrum in puppies and kittens. Animals, 2021. 11(11): p. 3260.

5. Case, L.P., The dog: its behavior, nutrition, and health. 2023: John Wiley & Sons.

6. Berschneider, H.M., Alternative diets. Clinical techniques in small animal practice, 2002. 17(1): p. 1-5.

7. Peterson, M.E., Care of the orphaned puppy and kitten. Small animal pediatrics. Philadelphia: WB Saunders, 2011: p. 67-72.

8. Brooks, D., et al., 2014 AAHA weight management guidelines for dogs and cats. Journal of the American Animal Hospital Association, 2014. 50(1): p. 1-11.

9. Oberbauer, A.M. and J.A. Larsen, Amino acids in dog nutrition and health. Amino Acids in Nutrition and Health: Amino Acids in the Nutrition of Companion, Zoo and Farm Animals, 2021: p. 199-216.

10. Erecinska, M., S. Cherian, and I.A. Silver, Energy metabolism in mammalian brain during development. Progress in neurobiology, 2004. 73(6): p. 397-445.

11. Stockman, J., C. Villaverde, and R.J. Corbee, Calcium, phosphorus, and vitamin D in dogs and cats: beyond the bones. Veterinary Clinics: Small Animal Practice, 2021. 51(3): p. 623-634.

12. Gácsi, M., et al., Species-specific differences and similarities in the behavior of hand- raised dog and wolf pups in social situations with humans. Developmental Psychobiology: The Journal of the International Society for Developmental Psychobiology, 2005. 47(2): p. 111-122.

13. Malm, K. and P. Jensen, Weaning in dogs: within-and between-litter variation in milk and solid food intake. Applied Animal Behavior Science, 1996. 49(3): p. 223-235.

14. Wells, D., Behavior of dogs. The ethology of domestic animals: an introductory text, 2017: p. 228-238.

15. Lawler, D., Neonatal and pediatric care of the puppy and kitten. Theriogenology, 2008. 70(3): p. 384-392.

16. Howell, T.J. and P.C. Bennett, Puppy power! Using social cognition research tasks to improve socialization practices for domestic dogs (Canis familiaris). Journal of Veterinary Behavior, 2011. 6(3): p. 195-204.

17. Case, L.P., et al., Canine and feline nutrition: a resource for companion animal professionals. 2010: Elsevier Health Sciences.

18. Cline, M.G., et al., 2021 AAHA nutrition and weight management guidelines for dogs and cats. Journal of the American Animal Hospital Association, 2021. 57(4): p. 153- 178.

19. Bourgeois, H., et al., Dietary behavior of dogs and cats. Bulletin de l'Académie vétérinaire de France, 2006. 159(4): p. 301-308.

20. Pieri, N.C.G., et al., Comparative development of embryonic age by organogenesis in domestic dogs and cats. Reproduction in Domestic Animals, 2015. 50(4): p. 625-631.

21. Johnson, C., Pregnancy management in the bitch. Theriogenology, 2008. 70(9): p. 1412-1417.

22. Council, N.R., Nutrient requirements of dogs and cats. 2006: National Academies Press.

PART 5. Management of Breed-Specific Nutritional Disorders in Dogs

Dogs come in a variety of breeds, each with its own set of characteristics, temperaments, and, surprisingly, nutritional needs [1]. Although nutrition is an important part of a dog's well-being, not all breeds have the same nutritional needs [2]. If a dog's diet does not take these characteristics into account, breed-specific nutritional problems can occur.

Having established that different dog breeds have unique health predispositions, let's delve deeper into the specifics of breed-specific nutritional disorders and how targeted dietary adjustments can prevent or alleviate these conditions.

Dogs can suffer from health issues if their food is deficient in vital elements or unbalanced [3]. Good nutrition is therefore essential for a dog's health and well-being.

This chapter discusses breed-specific nutritional problems in dogs, including their origins, treatments, and preventive measures. In order to control symptoms, minimize complications, aand improve affected dogs' overall fitness and well-being of affected dogs, these conditions often require specialized nutritional treatment.

Understanding Breed-Specific Nutritional Disorders

Breed-specific nutritional diseases occur when a dog's genetic makeup interacts with its diet, resulting in health problems that are more prevalent in certain breeds [4]. These diseases highlight the importance of tailoring a dog's diet to the specific needs of its breed.

Different breeds are genetically predisposed to certain health problems:

- **Giant and Large Breeds**
  Breeds such as Great Danes, Saint Bernards, and Irish Wolfhounds are prone to musculoskeletal disorders such as hip problems and arthritis [5].

- **Smaller Breeds**
  Breeds such as Dachshunds and Basset Hounds are more susceptible to disc degeneration due to their elongated spines [6].

A combination of genetic, physiological, and lifestyle factors contribute to the susceptibility of smaller and larger breeds to various health problems, such as dental disease and joint problems.

Larger Breeds and Joint Problems

Larger breeds carry more weight, which puts extra stress on their joints.

This can lead to joint deterioration or aggravate conditions such as hip dysplasia, a common problem in larger breeds. Hip Dysplasia is a genetic disorder primarily seen in larger dog breeds where the hip joint does not form properly, leading to arthritis and mobility issues.

Additionally, large breeds often grow rapidly, which can sometimes lead to joint and bone development problems. These problems can be exacerbated by inadequate or unbalanced nutrition during their rapid growth period.

Many large breeds are genetically predisposed to certain joint problems. For example, breeds such as German Shepherds and Labrador Retrievers are known to have a higher incidence of hip and elbow Dysplasia.

Smaller Breeds and Dental Diseases

Smaller breeds often have more crowded teeth due to their smaller mouths, leading to increased plaque and tartar buildup. This overcrowding can make it more difficult for them to clean their teeth naturally by chewing.

Dental diseases in small breeds often result from overcrowding of teeth, leading to greater accumulation of plaque and tartar, which, if not properly managed, can result in serious periodontal diseases.

Additionally, softer foods, as opposed to harder, crunchier ones that naturally clean teeth, often contribute to faster plaque buildup in smaller dogs.

Smaller breeds tend to have longer lifespans, which means their teeth are in use for longer periods, contributing to increased wear and a higher risk of dental problems over time.

Lifestyle and Grooming Factors

Nutritional requirements differ significantly between small and large breeds, and an unbalanced diet can contribute to these health problems.

Additionally, both over- and under-exercise can lead to health problems in dogs of different sizes:

- **Larger Dogs:** May be more likely to suffer from excessive exercise at a young age

- **Smaller Dogs:** May not get enough exercise to keep their bodies healthy

Understanding these breed-specific tendencies helps provide the appropriate care, nutrition, and medical attention to prevent or effectively manage these conditions. Imbalances in a dog's diet can lead to breed-specific nutritional disorders [7]. A deficiency of key nutrients or an overconsumption of others can cause these imbalances. Certain breeds are more susceptible to these disorders than others.

Let's take a closer look at some breed-specific nutritional disorders and their associated breeds.

Hip Dysplasia

Hip Dysplasia is a genetic disorder that affects the function and structure of the hip joint [8].

Causes

Heredity, rapid growth, and poor nutrition can all lead to joint problems. While heredity is important, diet can also influence the development and severity of hip Dysplasia [9]. Let's take a closer look:

- **Genetic Predisposition**
  Dogs often inherit hip Dysplasia from their parents due to its hereditary nature. Breeds such as German Shepherds, Labrador Retrievers, and Golden Retrievers are more prone to this condition. Genetic factors primarily cause hip dysplasia, which dogs often inherit from their parents. It is particularly prevalent in certain larger breeds due to their genetic makeup.

- **Rapid Growth and Nutrition**
  Puppies that grow too fast, especially large-breed puppies, can develop hip Dysplasia. Nutrition plays a crucial role in this, as diets that are too high in calories or have the wrong balance of calcium and phosphorus can promote rapid growth. Proper nutritional management, particularly during the rapid growth phases of large breed puppies, is crucial to prevent excessive weight and stress on developing joints, thereby reducing the risk of hip Dysplasia.

- **Levels of exercise and activity**
  Excessive or inappropriate exercise during a dog's growth can increase the risk of hip Dysplasia. Activities that put a lot of stress on the hips, such as jumping or repetitive movements on hard surfaces, can aggravate the condition.

- **Obesity**
  Being overweight puts extra stress on a dog's joints, including the hips. This can exacerbate the symptoms of hip Dysplasia or even increase the risk of developing it.

- **Incorrect Joint Formation**
  Sometimes the hip joint doesn't form properly during growth. The ball and socket of the hip may not fit together properly, leading to increased wear and tear.

- **Lifestyle Factors**
  Certain lifestyle factors, such as lack of exercise or over-exercising, can influence the development of hip Dysplasia.

- **Age-Related Degeneration**
  As dogs age, their joints naturally degenerate, which can lead to or worsen hip Dysplasia.

Symptoms

Understanding these causes helps us recognize the signs and symptoms of hip Dysplasia, which can vary in severity but typically manifest as follows:

- The hind legs may exhibit limping or lameness.

- There is difficulty in standing up, jumping, or climbing stairs.

- Audible clicking noise from the hip

- Decreased activity or reluctance to exercise

- Pain and stiffness

- The thigh muscles are experiencing a reduction in muscle mass.

Prevention

Identifying these symptoms early can lead to more effective management of the condition. Preventive measures are equally important to mitigate the risk or lessen the severity of hip Dysplasia:

- Avoid breeding dogs with a history of hip Dysplasia

- Ensure a balanced diet to prevent too-rapid growth in puppies, which can contribute to joint problems

- Maintain a regular exercise routine to keep muscles strong, but avoid overly strenuous activities that can stress the joints

Treatment

Weight control, physical therapy, joint supplements (such as glucosamine and chondroitin), and, in extreme situations, surgery are among the treatment options for hip Dysplasia.

To promote proper development, choose a large-breed pet food formula. Maintain a slender build to prevent joint stress.

Breeds

Great Danes, Saint Bernards, Irish Wolfhounds, and Rottweilers, as well as Labrador Retrievers, German Shepherds, and Golden Retrievers, are most susceptible to this condition.

Intervertebral Disc Disease (IVDD)

When the discs between a dog's vertebrae deteriorate or herniate, it causes back discomfort and movement problems [10].

IVDD involves the compression of spinal nerves caused by the failure of the cushioning discs, leading to pain, possible nerve damage, and varying degrees of paralysis.

Causes

- **Genetic Predisposition**
  Certain breeds are genetically predisposed to IVDD. Breeds at higher risk often have a type of disc degeneration that starts earlier in life.

- **Age**
  As dogs age, their discs naturally degenerate and lose their flexibility, making them more susceptible to injury and disease.

- **Physical Trauma**
  Traumatic events such as falls or accidents can cause or aggravate IVDD, especially in dogs that are already at risk.

- **Obesity**
  Overweight dogs are at a higher risk of IVDD because the extra weight puts more stress on the spine and intervertebral discs.

- **Lifestyle and Activity Level**
  Dogs who are very active or engage in intense physical activity may be more susceptible to spinal injuries that can lead to IVDD. Conversely, a lack of exercise can also contribute to poor spinal health.

- **Dietary Factors**
  Poor nutrition can affect the health of a dog's bones and joints, including the vertebrae and intervertebral discs.

- **Chronic Poor Posture**
  Certain postures or repetitive movements, often related to a dog's daily activities or sleeping habits, can put undue stress on the spine and contribute to disc degeneration.

Understanding these causes is crucial for recognizing the signs and managing the condition effectively. Let's examine the common symptoms that may indicate the presence of IVDD in a dog.

Symptoms

- Back pain and weakness.

- Reluctance to jump or move.

- Yelping with pain when touched or moved.

- Muscle spasms along the spine.

- Ataxia refers to a loss of coordination in the back legs (Ataxia means a lack of coordination. Dogs with Ataxia lose muscle control of their limbs. This can lead to a lack of balance, coordination, and gait problems).

- In severe cases, paralysis.

Recognizing these symptoms early can lead to timely interventions, which are crucial for preventing further complications. Now, let's explore how we can prevent IVDD from developing or worsening.

Prevention

- Keep your dog at a healthy weight to reduce stress on the spine

- Avoid activities that put undue stress on your dog's back, such as jumping from heights

- Provide a supportive bed to reduce stress on the spine

Treatment

Rest, anti-inflammatory medications, physical therapy, and, in rare cases, surgery to correct the herniated disc material may be used to treat IVDD.

- **Weight Control**
  Maintaining a healthy weight is essential to keeping the spine in good shape.

- **Dietary Treatment**
  Dachshunds are susceptible to IVDD because of their long spines. Dietary modifications can help reduce the risk and treat the condition. Dietary treatment for dogs with IVDD focuses on providing balanced nutrition that supports bone and joint health, incorporating essential nutrients that help maintain spinal integrity.

- **Joint Supplements**
  For joint health, use Glucosamine and Chondroitin tablets.

Breeds

The breeds that are more predisposed to IVDD are generally those with long backs and short legs, known as chondrodystrophic breeds, are generally more predisposed to IVDD. These include Dachshunds, Corgis, and Basset Hounds. These breeds are more likely to develop IVDD.

Note: Chondrodystrophic breeds are a specific group of dog breeds characterized by a distinctive body shape, including shorter legs and longer backs relative to body size. A form of dwarfism, particularly in the limbs, causes changes in cartilage and bone development, leading to this unique skeletal structure. "Chondro" refers to cartilage, and "Dystrophy" refers to a disorder of growth or development.

Dilated Cardiomyopathy (DCM)

Dilated cardiomyopathy is a cardiac disorder characterized by ventricular dilatation and impaired ventricular performance [11]. In dogs, DCM is a serious condition that affects the heart muscle, resulting in an enlarged heart and a reduced ability to pump blood effectively. With a basic understanding of DCM's impact on a dog's heart function, let's delve into the various factors that contribute to its development.

Causes

Researchers have linked the development of DCM to nutritional deficiencies, particularly Taurine deficiency. While the exact causes of DCM can vary, they generally fall into two categories: genetic and non-genetic.

- **Genetic Predisposition**
  Breeds that are more susceptible to DCM often inherit it. Breeds such as Doberman Pinschers, Great Danes, Irish Wolfhounds, and Boxers are known to have a higher genetic risk of developing DCM.

- **Dietary Factors**
  Dogs fed grain-free diets, diets high in legumes, or diets high in potatoes are particularly susceptible to DCM. These diets may lack certain amino acids, such as taurine, which is essential for heart health. Taurine is an amino acid that is essential for the proper function of cardiac muscle. Deficiencies in taurine can lead to weakened heart muscles, contributing significantly to the development of DCM. However, researchers are still studying and fully understanding the link between diet and DCM.

- **Age and Sex**
  Middle-aged to older dogs are more likely to develop DCM. There is also a slight gender predisposition, with males being more likely than females.

- **Infections**
  Certain viral or bacterial infections can cause myocarditis (inflammation of the heart muscle), which in some cases may contribute to the development of DCM.

- **Toxins and Drugs**
  Exposure to certain toxins or the use of certain drugs can sometimes lead to DCM. These cases are less common, but they can occur.

- **Underlying Metabolic Disorders**
  Some metabolic disorders, such as hypothyroidism or diabetes, can increase the risk of developing DCM.

- **Unknown Causes**
  Dogs with DCM often lack a specific cause, leading to its classification as idiopathic, meaning its causes are either unknown or poorly understood.

Knowing these causes helps us identify the symptoms of DCM, which are crucial for early diagnosis and effective management.

Symptoms

- Coughing

- Difficulty breathing

- Reduced exercise tolerance

- Weakness or lethargy

- Fainting or collapse

- Abdominal bloating due to fluid retention

Prevention

- Regular veterinary visits for early detection and treatment

- Ensure a balanced diet; be cautious of high-pulse or grain-free diets unless specifically recommended by a vet

- For breeds susceptible to DCM, consider genetic testing and consult a veterinarian for preventive strategies

Treatment

Treatment options may include medications to maintain heart function and dietary supplements containing taurine and other nutrients. Consult a veterinarian for nutritional advice, which may include appropriate supplementation.

Choose a Taurine-enriched dog food or one that meets the AAFCO (Association of American Feed Control Officials) Nutrient Profiles.

AAFCO Nutrient Profiles ensure that pet foods meet specified nutritional levels required to provide a complete and balanced diet for various stages of a dog's life, including specific formulations for those at risk of cardiac issues.

Breeds

Some breeds, such as Doberman Pinschers and Boxers, are genetically predisposed to DCM.

Obesity

Obesity, a growing concern among pets, can lead to other health problems such as diabetes, heart disease, and joint problems. Certain breeds, such as Labrador Retrievers and Beagles, are more susceptible to obesity due to their insatiable appetites.

Studies have linked obesity to various health problems such as diabetes, joint problems, and cardiovascular disease [12]. Given the significant impact of obesity on a dog's health, it's important to understand the various factors that contribute to this condition.

Causes

Simply put, an excess of calories consumed compared to energy expended causes obesity. Numerous factors, often involving a combination of lifestyle, genetic, and environmental influences, contribute to the growing concern of obesity in dogs. Here are the main causes:

- **Overfeeding**
  This is the most common cause of dog obesity. Providing too much food, too many treats, or too much human food can lead to an excessive calorie intake.

- **Lack of Exercise**
  Dogs that do not get enough exercise are more likely to gain weight. Exercise is essential for burning calories and maintaining a healthy weight. Regular exercise not only burns calories but also helps to maintain muscle tone, boost metabolism, and improve overall health, thereby playing a critical role in preventing obesity.

- **Age**
  Older dogs are less active, have slower metabolisms, and are more prone to weight gain than younger dogs.

- **Neutering or Spaying**
  Neutered or spayed dogs may have a lower metabolic rate, making them more susceptible to weight gain if their diet and exercise are not adjusted accordingly.

- **Breed Predisposition**
  Some breeds are more prone to obesity than others. For example, Labrador Retrievers, Beagles, and Dachshunds are breeds that tend to gain weight more easily.

- **Genetics**
  As with humans, some dogs may be genetically predisposed to obesity, which can affect their metabolism and appetite regulation.

- **Medical Conditions**
Certain health problems such as hypothyroidism or Cushing's disease can cause dogs to gain weight.

- **Medications**
Some medications, such as corticosteroids, may increase appetite and cause weight gain.

- **Owner's Lifestyle and Habits**
The lifestyle and habits of the dog's owner can have a significant impact on the pet's weight. Owners who are less active or tend to overfeed their pets often have dogs that are overweight or obese.

- **Owner's Lack of Knowledge or Awareness**
Sometimes dog owners do not recognize or understand what a healthy weight looks like for their dog, or they may not be aware of the correct portion sizes for their pet. Educating dog owners about the signs of obesity, proper feeding practices, and the importance of regular vet check-ups can significantly influence the health outcomes of their pets.

Recognizing these causal factors is critical to identifying the symptoms of obesity, which is important for early intervention. In addition, the symptoms are usually very clear.

Symptoms

- **Excess Body Fat**
A noticeable rise in body fat frequently manifests as a rounded or protruding abdomen.

- **Difficulty with Physical Activity or Exercise**
The dog exhibits listlessness and laziness. There is a decrease in stamina and a reluctance to participate in physical activities, even those he has always loved,

- **Shortness of Breath**
Even after mild exercise, one may experience heavy breathing or panting.

- **Sluggishness or Lethargy**
General lack of energy and enthusiasm.

- **Visible Difficulty Grooming**
Struggling to reach certain parts of the body during grooming.

Prevention

- **Feed a Balanced Diet**
Avoid overfeeding; measure food portions accurately, and limit treats.

- **Ensure Daily Physical Activity**
Regular exercise is essential to maintaining a healthy weight.

- **Monitor Weight Regularly**
Keep track of your dog's weight and overall condition through regular check-ups.

Treatment

Treatment of obesity requires a balanced diet, calorie restriction, frequent physical activity, and, in some circumstances, medication for weight management. Here are some specific strategies:

- **Switch to a Low-Calorie Diet**
  To effectively manage calorie intake, implement portion control.

- **Maximize Fiber Intake**
  Increase fiber in the diet to help your dog feel fuller longer.

- **Avoid High-Calorie Foods**
  Refrain from feeding table scraps, restaurant leftovers, or any high-calorie foods.

- **Establish a Regular Exercise Program**
  Develop a consistent exercise routine to help burn calories and maintain muscle tone.

Breeds

- **Labrador Retriever and Beagle**
  These breeds are particularly prone to obesity due to their insatiable appetites.

- **Chihuahua**
  Because of their small size, Chihuahuas can easily become overweight.

Pancreatitis

Some small breeds, such as Miniature Schnauzers and Yorkshire Terriers, are prone to pancreatitis, or swelling of the pancreas [13]. In these breeds, a high-fat diet can cause pancreatitis, abdominal discomfort, vomiting, and diarrhea. Now that we understand which breeds are more susceptible to pancreatitis, let's explore the various factors that can trigger this painful condition.

Causes

Numerous factors can cause pancreatitis in dogs, an inflammation of the pancreas. Understanding these causes is critical for the condition's prevention and effective treatment. Here are the main causes:

- **High-Fat Diet**
  The consumption of high-fat foods is a significant risk factor. This includes both high-fat dog foods and high-fat human foods, such as table scraps. A sudden increase in fat intake can be particularly problematic. A high-fat diet can lead to the accumulation of fat in the cells of the pancreas, which interferes with its normal function and can trigger inflammation.

- **Obesity**
  Overweight dogs have a higher risk of developing pancreatitis. Excess body fat can alter metabolism and increase inflammation, contributing to the condition.

- **Age and Breed**
  Although pancreatitis can occur in any dog, certain breeds, such as Miniature Schnauzers, are more susceptible. Older dogs are also at higher risk.

- **Certain Medications**
  Some medications, such as corticosteroids or certain diuretics, can increase the risk of pancreatitis.

- **Abdominal Trauma**
  An jInjury to the abdomen, such as from a car accident or a fall, can damage the pancreas and lead to pancreatitis.

- **Metabolic Disorders**
  Conditions such as Hypercalcemia (high levels of calcium in the blood) or Hyperlipidemia (high levels of fat in the blood) can contribute to the development of Pancreatitis.

- **Idiopathic Causes**
  In many cases, the exact cause of Pancreatitis in dogs is unknown. This is known as idiopathic pancreatitis.

- **Infections**
  Certain viral or bacterial infections can contribute to the development of Pancreatitis.

- **Underlying Health Conditions**
  Diseases that affect fat metabolism or the endocrine system, such as diabetes mellitus, can be risk factors for Pancreatitis.

- **Genetic Factors**
  There may be a genetic predisposition in some dogs, although this is less well understood than other factors.

Now that the factors that lead to pancreatitis are known, it is important to recognize the symptoms early to ensure timely and effective treatment. Again, the symptoms are simple to identify. Let's see what they are.

Symptoms

- **Abdominal Pain**
  The dog might hunch over in discomfort.

- **Vomiting**
  Frequent vomiting can be a sign of pancreatitis.

- **Diarrhea**
  Loose stools or diarrhea are common symptoms.

- **Loss of Appetite**
  Affected dogs often refuse to eat.

- **Lethargy**
  General lack of energy and enthusiasm.

- **Dehydration**
  Dehydration may occur due to vomiting and diarrhea.

Prevention

- **Feed a Low-Fat Diet**
  To prevent the condition from arising, avoid fatty table scraps.

- **Maintain a Regular Exercise Routine**
  Regular physical activity helps maintain a healthy weight and reduces risk factors.

- **Introduce New Foods Gradually**
  It is important to gradually ensure that the dog's digestive system can adapt without overwhelming the pancreas, thereby reducing the risk of Pancreatitis.

Treatment

Treatment includes dietary changes, such as a low-fat diet, and medications to control swelling and discomfort [14].

Avoid giving out fatty foods or table scraps. Administer multiple small meals throughout the day to reduce stress on the pancreas.

If a dog shows symptoms such as vomiting, abdominal pain, or lethargy, it's important to seek immediate veterinary attention, as pancreatitis can be a serious, potentially life-threatening condition.

Breeds

Miniature Schnauzer and Yorkshire Terrier.

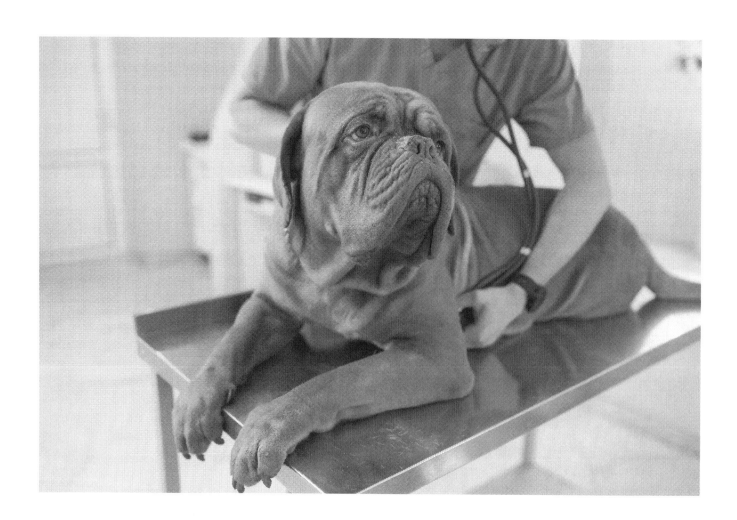

Dental Diseases

Dental disease is very common in dogs, especially as they get older. It involves the build-up of plaque, which leads to inflamed gums and tooth decay. Poor nutrition can exacerbate dental problems in dogs, such as gum disease and tooth decay [15].

To tackle dental diseases effectively, it's crucial to understand the underlying causes that contribute to these conditions.

Causes

Dental disease in dogs, often referred to as periodontal disease, is a common problem that can have several contributing factors. Poor dental hygiene and specific diets can contribute to dental problems. Dental disease in dogs can be caused by various factors.

- **Poor Oral Hygiene**
  This is the number one cause of dental disease. Without regular brushing or dental care, plaque builds up on the teeth and hardens into tartar, which can lead to gum disease and tooth decay.

- **Age**
  Due to increased wear and potential neglect over the years, older dogs are more prone to dental disease.

- **Breed Size and Genetics**
  Small breeds and brachycephalic breeds (such as Bulldogs and Pugs) are more prone to dental problems due to overcrowding of teeth. Genetics can also play a role in a dog's susceptibility to dental problems.

- **Diet**
  Soft or sticky foods can contribute to plaque build-up. Diets that do not mechanically clean teeth can increase the risk of dental disease.

- **Chewing Behavior**
  Dogs that don't chew much or don't have access to chew toys that help clean their teeth may be at higher risk of developing dental problems.

- **Lack of Professional Dental Care**
  Regular professional cleanings by a veterinarian are important for maintaining oral health. These cleanings play a crucial role in eliminating tartar that brushing alone cannot eliminate, thereby preventing periodontal disease and its complications.

- **Underlying Health Problems**
Certain systemic diseases, such as diabetes, can contribute to the development of dental disease.

- **Misaligned Teeth or Bite Problems**
Dogs with misaligned teeth may have more difficulty keeping their teeth clean, leading to an increased risk of dental disease.

- **Poor Nutrition**
Especially during development, poor nutrition can lead to weaker teeth and gums, making them more susceptible to disease.

- **Certain Medications**
Some medications can affect oral health or reduce the flow of saliva, which has a natural cleansing effect on the teeth.

Symptoms

- **Bad Breath (Halitosis)**
Persistent bad breath can indicate dental disease.

- **Red, Swollen or Bleeding Gums**
Inflamed gums are a common sign of periodontal disease.

- **Difficulty Eating or Loss of Appetite**
Dental pain can make eating uncomfortable for dogs.

- **Pawing at the Mouth or Face**
Dogs may paw at their mouths if they are experiencing dental discomfort.

- **Loose or Missing Teeth**
Advanced dental disease can cause teeth to become loose or fall out.

- **Drooling that may be Blood-Colored**
Excessive drooling, especially if tinged with blood, can indicate dental issues.

Prevention

These factors are included in the prevention of dental disease in dogs:

- **Regular Brushing**
With dog toothpaste, brush your dog's teeth on a regular basis.

- **Dental-Friendly Chew Toys**
Provide chew toys that help clean teeth and massage gums.

- **A Diet that Supports Dental Health**
Feed a diet specifically designed to promote dental health, such as kibble that helps reduce plaque buildup.

- **Regular Veterinary Check-Ups**
  Ensure regular check-ups that include dental assessments.

Schedule regular visits to the veterinarian to check the teeth. Early intervention and consistent dental care are critical to preventing serious dental problems in dogs.

Treatment

- **Dental-Specific Meals or Chews**
  Use dental-specific meals or dental chews to help clean teeth.

- **Regular Brushing**
  Brush your dog's teeth on a regular basis or give him oral care snacks.

- **Diet for Dental Health**
  Feed a diet that helps maintain dental health by choosing high-quality food.

Breeds

- **Toy Breeds**
  Chihuahuas, Yorkshire Terriers, and Pomeranians are more susceptible to dental problems due to overcrowded teeth, which can contribute to tartar buildup and Periodontitis.

- **Brachycephalic Breeds**
  The shape of their jaws often compresses the teeth of dogs with small muzzles, like Bulldogs, Pugs, and Shih Tzus, making them more susceptible to dental issues.

- **Dachshunds**
  Because of their long, narrow jaws, they may have more crowded teeth, increasing the potential for dental disease.

- **Chihuahuas**
  Because Chihuahuas have relatively small mouths, they are more likely to experience dental overcrowding, which can result in issues such as tartar accumulation, gum disease, and tooth loss at an earlier age.

- **Bichon Frises**
  Due to their small mouths, Bichon Frises are prone to dental overcrowding and associated problems such as tartar buildup, gum disease, and tooth loss.

Note: Brachycephalic breeds are dogs that have a short, broad skull, giving them a "flat-faced" or "snub-nosed" appearance. This facial structure is due to a genetic trait that alters the proportions of their skull, resulting in a shorter than normal muzzle. "Brachy" means "shortened," while "cephalic" refers to the head.

Urinary Stones (Urolithiasis)

Dietary variables may influence the development of urolithiasis [16]. Understanding the dietary and physiological factors that lead to urolithiasis is crucial for effective prevention and management.

Causes

Urinary stones, or Urolithiasis, in dogs are caused by the formation of mineral deposits in the urinary tract. Improper diet and several factors contribute to the development of these stones:

- **Dietary Mineral Imbalance**
  Certain diets can increase the risk of stone formation by affecting urine pH and mineral balance. Diets high in certain minerals, such as calcium, phosphorus, or magnesium, can contribute to stone formation.

- **Urinary pH Imbalance**
  The pH of a dog's urine is critical for stone formation. A urine pH that is too acidic or too alkaline can lead to the formation of different types of stones.

- **Chronic Dehydration or Low Water Intake**
  Inadequate water intake can lead to more concentrated urine, which increases the risk of mineral crystals forming into stones.

- **Urinary Tract Infections (UTIs)**
  Some types of urinary stones, particularly struvite stones, are associated with bacterial infections of the urinary tract. Magnesium Ammonium Phosphate is the main mineral that forms struvite stones. In dogs, the formation of struvite stones is often associated with certain pathological conditions. The pH of the urine and the presence of certain bacteria heavily influence the formation of struvite stones, making them particularly responsive to dietary management.

- **Genetic Predisposition**
  Some breeds are more prone to developing certain types of urinary stones. For example, Dalmatians are known to be prone to urate stones due to a genetic variation affecting uric acid metabolism.

- **Underlying Medical Conditions**
  Dogs with liver disease or calcium metabolism disorders are more likely to develop stones.

- **Medications**
  Certain medications can alter the composition of the urine or the health of the urinary tract, leading to stone formation.

- **Age and Sex**
  Older dogs and certain genders (depending on the type of stone) may be more prone to developing stones. For example, male dogs are generally more prone to urethral blockage due to stones.

- **Sedentary Lifestyle, or Obesity**
  A sedentary lifestyle or obesity can contribute to urinary stone formation due to changes in metabolism and urinary congestion.

- **Dietary Changes**
  Sudden changes in diet can alter the composition of urine, potentially leading to stone formation.

These factors, if not managed properly, can manifest as a range of symptoms that indicate the presence of urinary stones.

Symptoms

- **Blood in the Urine**
  Presence of blood can indicate irritation or injury caused by stones.

- **Straining or Vocalizing when Urinating**
  Difficulty or pain during urination.

- **Frequent Loss of Small Amounts of Urine**
  The patient frequently urinates, yet only manages to pass minimal volumes.

- **Accidents or Urinating in Unusual Places**
  Discomfort causes changes in urination habits.

- **Abdominal Pain**
  Abdominal pain may indicate the presence of stones.

- **Lethargy or Loss of Appetite**
  Reduced energy levels and a lack of interest in food.

Prevention

- **Dietary Management:** Use food to control the mineral composition and pH of the urine and to feed a diet that prevents the formation of stones.

- **Ensure Adequate Hydration:** To dilute the urine, maintain proper hydration, which reduces the concentration of minerals that can form stones.

- **Regular Veterinary Checks:** To monitor urinary health and identify problems early, regular check-ups are necessary.

Treatment

- **Specific Kidney Health Diet**
  Feed a veterinarian-recommended diet designed to support kidney health and prevent stone formation.

- **Ensure Adequate Hydration**
  Always provide clean water to ensure your dog stays well-hydrated.

- **Surgery**
  In some cases, surgery may be required to remove the stones.

- **Regular Monitoring and Veterinary Care**
  Regular check-ups and monitoring are essential for dogs prone to urinary stones.

Breeds

- **Dalmatian:** This breed has a hereditary susceptibility to inadequate liver metabolism, which can result in uric acid in the urine.

- **Miniature Schnauzer:** Urinary tract infections or nutritional issues may cause stones.

- **English Bulldog:** They are susceptible to Calcium Oxalate crystal formation, especially if their diet is high in Oxalate-containing foods.

Diabetes Mellitus

Dogs can develop diabetes, which is often associated with obesity. Managing this condition requires lifelong attention to diet and insulin therapy. Obesity and an improper diet can exacerbate diabetes [17].

Numerous factors can cause diabetes in dogs, making it a chronic condition. There are two main types of canine diabetes:

1. **Diabetes Mellitus:** Similar to Type 1 Diabetes in humans, involves insufficient insulin production.

2. **Diabetes Insipidus:** Is a rarer condition characterized by an imbalance in water metabolism, leading to excessive urination and thirst.

Understanding these two different types of diabetes will help us explore their specific causes and the strategies needed to manage them effectively.

But let's take a closer look:

Causes of Diabetes Mellitus

- **Autoimmune Destruction of Pancreatic Cells**
  The most common cause in dogs is immune-mediated destruction of insulin-producing cells in the pancreas, similar to type 1 diabetes in humans.

- **Genetic Predisposition**
  Certain breeds are more prone to developing diabetes, suggesting a genetic component. For example, Australian Terriers, Samoyeds, and Miniature Schnauzers have higher rates of the disease.

- **Obesity**
  Overweight dogs are more likely to develop diabetes because obesity can lead to insulin resistance. Insulin resistance occurs when a dog's body fails to respond normally to insulin, necessitating higher levels of insulin to maintain blood glucose control. This condition often precedes the development of Diabetes Mellitus.

- **Pancreatic Injury or Disease**
  Conditions that damage the pancreas, such as pancreatitis or pancreatic tumors, can lead to diabetes by affecting insulin production.

- **Age**
  Diabetes can occur at any age, but it is more common in older dogs.

- **Hormonal Imbalances**
Conditions like Cushing's disease (Hyperadrenocorticism) or the use of certain hormones, such as progesterone, can interfere with insulin regulation.

- **Poor Diet and Lack of Exercise**
A diet high in fat and carbohydrates, combined with a lack of exercise, can contribute to obesity and insulin resistance, increasing the risk of diabetes.

Causes of Diabetes Insipidus

- **Deficiency of Antidiuretic Hormone (ADH)**
ADH deficiency, also known as vasopressin, causes this rare form of Diabetes in dogs by regulating water absorption in the kidneys.

- **Damage to the Pituitary Gland or Hypothalamus**
Trauma, tumors, or congenital defects affecting the areas of the brain that produce ADH can lead to diabetes insipidus.

The manifestation of these causes in daily life can lead to a range of symptoms that can have a significant impact on a dog's health.

So it is very important to recognize these signs immediately and with certainty:

Symptoms of Diabetes Insipidus

- **Increased Thirst and Urination**
Dogs may drink and urinate excessively due to their inability to concentrate urine.

- **Weight Loss with Normal or Increased Appetite**
Despite having a normal or increased appetite, dogs may lose weight.

- **Lethargy**
General fatigue and a lack of energy can be observed.

- **Cloudy Eyes (especially in Dogs with Diabetes Mellitus)**
Dogs with diabetes mellitus are more likely to exhibit this symptom, but severe cases of diabetes insipidus can also cause it.

- **Recurrent Infections**
Frequent infections, particularly urinary tract infections, may occur.

Increased thirst and urination, weight loss, and changes in appetite should prompt a veterinary visit.

Prevention

- Maintain a healthy weight to reduce the risk of insulin resistance.

- Choose a balanced diet and avoid excess carbohydrates and sugar.

- Engage in regular physical activity to help regulate blood sugar levels.

- Regular check-ups and a healthy lifestyle can help prevent diabetes or manage it effectively if it does occur. Regular veterinary check-ups can lead to early detection of not only diabetes but also other underlying conditions that could exacerbate or trigger diabetic symptoms in dogs.

Treatment

Early diagnosis and treatment are essential in the management of diabetes in dogs. With the assistance of a veterinarian, ensure regular feeding. Select a good diabetic-friendly diet with limited carbohydrate intake. Monitor your blood glucose levels as directed.

Management of Diabetes Mellitus typically includes insulin therapy, dietary control, and regular exercise. Monitoring blood glucose levels is crucial to managing the condition. For diabetes insipidus, treatment depends on the underlying cause but often includes hormone replacement therapy.

Breeds

- **Pug:** Pugs have an increased risk of developing diabetes due to their tendency toward obesity.

- **Beagle:** Beagles are at risk because of their passion for food, which often leads to weight gain.

- **Poodles:** Miniature and Toy Poodles may be at risk due to their genetic predisposition.

Skin and Coat Problems

Dogs can suffer from various skin conditions, including allergies, infections, and hot spots. Nutritional deficiencies may cause skin and coat problems [18].

To effectively address these issues, it is crucial to understand the diverse causes that can contribute to skin and coat problems in dogs.

Causes

A variety of factors, including environmental influences, underlying health issues, and often nutritional deficiencies, can cause skin and coat problems in dogs. Understanding these causes is essential for effective treatment and prevention. Here are the main causes:

- **Allergies:** Allergic reactions are a common cause of skin problems in dogs. Food ingredients, environmental allergens like pollen or dust mites, or flea bites (Flea Allergic Dermatitis) can trigger allergies.

- **Parasites:** Fleas, ticks, mites, and lice can all cause skin irritation and lead to secondary infections. For example, mites can cause mange, which can significantly affect a dog's skin and coat.

- **Infections:** Bacterial, fungal (such as ringworm), and yeast infections can cause skin irritation, inflammation, and coat problems.

- **Nutritional Deficiencies:** A poor diet lacking essential nutrients, fatty acids, and vitamins can lead to a dull coat and unhealthy skin.

- **Hormonal Imbalances:** Conditions such as hypothyroidism or Cushing's disease can affect the skin and coat. Hypothyroidism often results in a dull coat and scaly skin, while Cushing's disease can cause thinning of the skin and hair loss.

- **Environmental Factors:** Exposure to harsh weather, irritants such as certain shampoos or grooming products, and swimming in chlorinated pools can affect a dog's skin and coat.

- **Genetics:** Certain skin conditions are more common in certain breeds. For example, oily skin in Cocker Spaniels can lead to seborrhoea. Seborrhoea in dogs is a skin condition characterized by excessive production of sebum, an oily substance produced by the skin's sebaceous glands. The condition can be primary (inherited) or secondary (caused by underlying health problems). Seborrhoea is particularly challenging due to its chronic nature and the discomfort it causes, making understanding its two forms—Oleosa and Sicca—essential for proper management.

- ○ **Seborrhoea Oleosa:** In this form, the skin produces excess sebum, resulting in oily, greasy skin and coat. The excess oil can cause a strong odor and the appearance of scaly, yellowish flakes.

- ○ **Seborrhoea Sicca:** This form is characterized by dry, scaly skin. The dog's skin may be itchy and irritated, as well as scaling and flaking.

- **Stress and Anxiety:** As with humans, tension and anxiety can affect a dog's skin and coat health.

- **Underlying Diseases:** Certain systemic diseases, such as liver or kidney disease, can manifest as skin problems.

- **Autoimmune Diseases:** Some autoimmune diseases, including Lupus and Pemphigus, can cause skin problems.

- **Grooming and Care:** Improper or infrequent grooming can lead to a variety of skin and coat problems, including matting, which can cause skin irritation.

These factors can manifest themselves in a variety of symptoms that are critical to properly recognizing and diagnosing various hair and skin conditions in dogs. Always observe your dog closely, and if you notice any of these signs, contact your veterinarian immediately for appropriate treatment.

Symptoms

- Itching and scratching

- The skin's redness or inflammation

- Dry, flaky, or greasy skin

- Hair loss or a thinning coat

- Foul skin odor

- Scabs, bumps, or rashes present

Prevention

Preventing skin and coat problems depends on the underlying cause. It's important to provide a balanced diet, regular grooming, and parasite control.

A diet enriched with essential fatty acids, particularly Omega-3 and Omega-6, plays a crucial role in maintaining skin barrier function and reducing inflammatory responses in the skin. If skin problems persist, a veterinary examination is necessary to determine the cause and appropriate treatment. Here are some tips:

- Always choose a balanced diet rich in essential fatty acids

- Regular grooming and bathing with appropriate products are crucial

- Regular use of flea and tick control products is important

- Keep your home clean and reduce allergens

Treatment

Treatment may include medication, dietary changes, or special grooming products. For healthy skin, choose a dog food that contains a balanced mix of Omega-3 and Omega-6 fatty acids. To promote a healthy coat, consider using supplements such as fish oil.

Breeds

- **Bulldogs, Labrador Retrievers, and Golden Retrievers:** Often suffer from food allergies and sensitivities, which can manifest as skin problems such as itching, rashes, and hair loss.

- **Bulldog:** Bulldogs with skin folds or wrinkles may be more susceptible to Dermatitis if their skin is not properly cleaned and groomed.

- **Dachshund or Greyhound:** Coat dullness or alopecia (hair loss) can occur if they lack certain nutrients in their diet.

- **West Highland White Terrier:** Prone to skin allergies.

- **Shar-Pei:** Prone to skin fold dermatitis.

- **Labrador Retriever:** Prone to atopic Dermatitis.

- **Cocker Spaniel:** Prone to Seborrhoea.

- **Bichon Frises:** They may suffer from a variety of skin conditions, often due to allergies, including atopic Dermatitis. Bichon Frises' fluffy and curly hair can make them susceptible to ear infections, particularly if they don't receive regular ear cleanings.

Management and Prevention Strategies for Canine Breed-Specific Nutritional Disorders

Now that we've looked at the most common breed-specific diseases, let's examine the treatment and management of these conditions in general. Managing breed-specific nutritional problems often involves a combination of dietary adjustments, medications, and lifestyle changes [19]. Effective management begins with the right diet tailored to each breed's unique needs.

1. **Dietary Changes:** Adjust the dog's diet to meet the breed's individual nutritional needs. This may include:

   - Selecting a commercial, breed-specific dog food that adheres to nutritional guidelines is crucial. Breed-specific dog foods formulate with the nutritional profiles of specific breeds in mind, directly addressing common health issues through tailored nutrient ratios.

   - Changing macronutrient ratios to address specific health concerns (e.g., reducing fat intake in breeds prone to pancreatitis).

   - Consider implementing specialized diets tailored for particular health conditions like inflammation and joint or cardiovascular health.

2. **Dietary Supplements:** In some cases, dietary supplements can play a critical role in therapy. Glucosamine and Chondroitin for joint health and taurine for heart health, are common supplements [20]. Always consult a veterinarian when adding supplements to a diet plan.

3. **Medications:** Veterinarians may prescribe medications to relieve pain, inflammation, or ongoing health issues associated with breed-specific nutritional diseases [21]. These medications can help alleviate symptoms and improve the dog's overall quality of life.

4. **Weight Control:** Weight control is critical for breeds prone to obesity or musculoskeletal problems [22]. Maintaining a healthy body weight through diet and exercise can help prevent joint pain and avoid weight-related health issues.

Preventive Measures

Preventing breed-specific nutritional problems is often easier than treating them. Here are some preventive measures to consider:

1. **Choose the Right Food:** Select a high-quality commercial dog food that is appropriate for your dog's breed, age, and activity level. Consult a veterinarian to determine the optimal diet for your particular breed.

2. **Portion Management:** Overeating can exacerbate various breed-specific health conditions. Follow the nutritional guidelines on the dog food packaging and adjust portions based on your dog's individual needs.

3. **Exercise Regularly:** Daily exercise helps your dog maintain a healthy weight and improves overall health and emotional well-being [23].

4. **Get Regular Veterinary Checkups:** Schedule frequent appointments with your veterinarian to evaluate your dog's health. Early detection of breed-specific diseases can improve the effectiveness of management and treatment. Regular veterinary check-ups are essential for monitoring health changes over time and enabling early intervention, which can significantly alter the course of breed-specific conditions.

5. **Genetic Analysis:** If you're considering getting a purebred dog, research the breed's tendencies and explore genetic testing to identify any potential health problems [24]. This information can help you determine your dog's nutritional and medical needs.

Focus On

Certain breeds are genetically predisposed to specific diseases. However, it's important to note that although these breeds are more prone to certain conditions, that doesn't mean that every dog of that breed will develop them. Regular veterinary check-ups, a healthy lifestyle, and preventative care are essential to managing the health of all dogs, regardless of breed.

Breed-specific nutritional problems in dogs highlight the importance of recognizing each breed's individual nutritional needs. Dog owners can reduce the risk of these diseases and provide a better, longer life by tailoring their dog's diet to its breed's unique needs. Veterinary advice is essential to ensure that your dog receives the proper nutrition and treatment for breed-specific health issues.

By combining proper nutrition, regular activity, and consistent veterinary care, you can help your dog thrive and live a healthy and happy life.

References

1. Rooney, N.J. and D.R. Sargan, Welfare concerns associated with pedigree dog breeding in the UK. Animal Welfare, 2010. 19(S1): p. 133-140.

2. Council, N.R., Nutrient requirements of dogs and cats. 2006: National Academies Press.

3. Jones, A., Canine and feline nutrition. The Complete Textbook of Veterinary Nursing2: The Complete Textbook of Veterinary Nursing, 2011: p. 121.

4. Dutton, E. and J. López-Alvarez, An update on canine cardiomyopathies–is it all in the genes? Journal of Small Animal Practice, 2018. 59(8): p. 455-464.

5. Mele, E., Epidemiology of osteoarthritis. Veterinary focus, 2007. 17(3): p. 4-10.

6. Packer, R.M., et al., How long and low can you go? Effect of conformation on the risk of thoracolumbar intervertebral disc extrusion in domestic dogs. PloS one, 2013. 8(7): p. e69650.

7. KĘPIŃSKA-PACELIK, J. and W. BIEL, NUTRITIONAL PROBLEMS OF LARGE AND GIANT BREED DOGS. PART I. PUPPIES. Folia Pomeranae Universitatis Technologiae Stetinensis Agricultura Alimentaria Piscaria et Zootechnica, 2023. 366(65).

8. Zhou, Z., et al., Differential genetic regulation of canine hip dysplasia and osteoarthritis. PloS one, 2010. 5(10): p. e13219.

9. Morgan, J.P., A. Wind, and A.P. Davidson, Hereditary bone and joint diseases in the dog: osteochondroses, hip dysplasia, elbow dysplasia. 2000: Schlütersche.

10. Jeffery, N., et al., Intervertebral disk degeneration in dogs: consequences, diagnosis, treatment, and future directions. Journal of veterinary internal medicine, 2013. 27(6): p. 1318-1333.

11. Bonagura, J. and L. Visser, Echocardiographic assessment of dilated cardiomyopathy in dogs. Journal of Veterinary Cardiology, 2022. 40: p. 15-50.

12. German, A.J., The growing problem of obesity in dogs and cats. The Journal of nutrition, 2006. 136(7): p. 1940S-1946S.

13. Bishop, M.A., Investigation Into Possible Mutations of the SPINK1 Gene as a Cause of Hereditary Pancreatitis in the Miniature Schnauzer. 2015.

14. Watson, P., Pancreatitis in dogs and cats: definitions and pathophysiology. Journal of small animal practice, 2015. 56(1): p. 3-12.

15. Gawor, J.P., et al., Influence of diet on oral health in cats and dogs. The Journal of nutrition,

2006. 136(7): p. 2021S-2023S.

16. Queau, Y., Nutritional management of urolithiasis. Veterinary Clinics: Small Animal Practice, 2019. 49(2): p. 175-186.

17. Rucinsky, R., et al., AAHA Diabetes management guidelines for dogs and cats. Journal of the American Animal Hospital Association, 2010. 46(3): p. 215-224.

18. Hensel, P., Nutrition and skin diseases in veterinary medicine. Clinics in dermatology, 2010. 28(6): p. 686-693.

19. Wallis, L.J., et al., Demographic change across the lifespan of pet dogs and their impact on health status. Frontiers in veterinary science, 2018: p. 200.

20. Li, P. and G. Wu, Amino acid nutrition and metabolism in domestic cats and dogs. Journal of Animal Science and Biotechnology, 2023. 14(1): p. 1-21.

21. Thorpe-Vargas, S. and M. John Cargill, Treatment of this disease must be tailored specifically to the needs of your pet, whether using conventional or alternative medicine.

22. Lund, E.M., et al., Prevalence and risk factors for obesity in adult dogs from private US veterinary practices. International Journal of Applied Research in Veterinary Medicine, 2006. 4(2): p. 177.

23. Hurley, K.J., D.A. Elliott, and E. Lund, Dog obesity, dog walking, and dog health. The health benefits of dog walking for pets and people: evidence and case studies, 2011. 125.

24. Burns, K., Unlocking the genetic secrets of your dog. 2018, Am Vet Med Assoc.

PART 6. Balanced Recipes for Healthy and Happy Dogs

The recipes and nutritional advice presented in this section of the book are intended for healthy dogs only and should not be used as a substitute for veterinary advice. The goal is to offer nutritious recipes that combine healthy ingredients with a simple preparation process that is within everyone's reach and doesn't require special utensils.

The suggested recipes aim to vary the main sources of protein and carbohydrates, which helps prevent food sensitivities and nutritional imbalances. Before making any significant changes to your dog's diet, especially if they have pre-existing medical conditions, it is essential to consult your veterinarian.

Given the complexity of prescribing a specific diet for dogs with medical conditions without a direct and detailed examination, this section only suggests generally healthy recipes and provides general nutritional advice. It is crucial to customize each dish according to the dog's age, weight, preferences, and any intolerances. Also, remember to consider your dog's individual energy needs, which may vary based on age, activity level, and health.

Each dog is unique, and his or her health may require a specific, individualized nutritional approach that should be discussed and monitored by a qualified professional. It is important to reiterate: always check the suitability of any diet or treatment with your pet's veterinarian. Following recipes or advice without proper veterinary supervision may be detrimental to your dog's health. With these general guidelines in mind, let's explore how to calculate your dog's specific dietary requirements.

General Considerations

To calculate the amount of food to feed your dog, you must consider their average caloric needs based on factors such as weight, age, activity level, and any specific health conditions or dietary needs.

Here's a brief overview of how to consider these factors:

1. **Weight**
   The basic guideline for caloric intake usually starts with the dog's weight. Different weight categories (small, medium, large, and extra-large) have different caloric needs. For example, small breeds typically need more calories per pound compared to larger breeds due to their faster metabolism.

2. **Age**
   Puppies, adult dogs, and senior dogs have different metabolic rates and nutritional needs. Puppies require more calories per kilogram of body weight for growth and development, whereas older dogs may need fewer calories to prevent weight gain due to a slower metabolism.

3. **Activity Level**

Active dogs, such as those that regularly engage in high-energy activities or are working dogs, require more calories than more sedentary animals. Conversely, a less active dog will need fewer calories to avoid obesity.

4. **Special Health Conditions and Needs**

Dogs with special health conditions (e.g., Diabetes, kidney disease) or those on a weight management plan may have unique dietary needs. These might include lower or higher caloric intake, specific nutrients, or medically prescribed diets. For instance, managing macronutrient intake carefully is crucial for dogs with Diabetes or kidney disease to avoid exacerbating their condition.

5. **Individual Variability**

Each dog has a unique metabolic rate and may process calories differently, even among dogs of the same age, breed, and size. It is important to monitor your dog's body condition and adjust food portions accordingly. Regularly assess your dog's weight and physical condition to ensure they remain within a healthy range.

Understanding these factors is just the first step; next, we need to delve into how these considerations influence the daily nutritional needs of your dog. By taking a comprehensive approach to your dog's diet, you can ensure they receive the proper nutrition to maintain their health and well-being.

The Importance of Estimating Daily Nutritional Needs

It is important to adjust food amounts based not only on your dog's weight but also on their age, activity level, and health. Active dogs may need more calories to meet their energy needs, while less active or older dogs may need fewer calories. Therefore, adjust the suggested recipes to the most appropriate nutritional values for your dog.

Always consult your veterinarian to ensure that your dog's diet meets their specific nutritional needs, especially if your dog has dietary restrictions or health problems.

Regular evaluation of your dog's body condition and weight adjustments can help maintain their overall health and well-being.

1. **Small Dogs (10-20 pounds or 4.5-9 kg):** Small dogs typically need about 200-400 calories per day. For puppies and active adult dogs, aim for the upper end of this range to meet their energy needs. Older dogs, unless very active, generally require fewer calories, so adjust portions toward the lower end of the range to avoid weight gain.

2. **Medium Dogs (20-50 pounds or 9-22.5 kg):** Medium dogs generally require about 400-700 calories per day. Puppies and very active dogs, such as those who frequently participate in agility or other high-energy activities, may require calories closer to the high end, while less active or older dogs should consume calories toward the low end to maintain optimal health.

3. **Large Dogs (50-90 pounds or 22.5-40 kg):** Large breed dogs require 700-1100 calories per day. Growing large large-breed and active working dogs may need more calories to support their larger bodies and higher energy levels, while older or less active dogs may benefit from fewer calories to help manage weight and joint health.

4. **Extra-Large Dogs (over 90 pounds or over 40 kg):** These dogs may require more than 1100 calories per day, especially if they are very active or working breeds. It is important to monitor their diets closely to ensure that they do not consume too much, which can lead to obesity, especially in less active or older extra-large dogs.

Consultation with your veterinarian is always necessary to provide individualized nutritional advice and help monitor your dog's health to ensure that their diet supports their overall well-being.

Summary of Ingredients

Listed below is a list of the ingredients that we use in our recipe, along with the reasons why these ingredients are helpful for canines. The use of these ingredients ensures that the recipes are not only healthy but also well-balanced and free of any potential risks that could be considered harmful to dogs.

This is something you should keep in mind when preparing homemade foods for your dog.

Meat and Fish

- **Chicken:** Because it is a lean source of protein, it aids in muscle development. Please make sure that it is boneless and cooked thoroughly to prevent any potential choking problems.

- **Turkey:** The advantages include a low-fat source of protein and a suitable substitute for dogs that are allergic to chicken. Use lean meat of excellent quality to maintain a low fat level.

- **Beef:** It is rich in essential amino acids and proteins for the body. If you want to prevent additional fat, use lean cuts.

- **Salmon:** The benefits include a high content of omega-3 fatty acids, which promote healthy skin and coat. Ensure it is fully cooked and devoid of any bones.

- **White Fish:** It provides a source of protein that is low in fat and abundant in Omega-3 fatty acids. Remove all bones as a precaution against potential choking issues.

Carbohydrates and Fiber

- **Brown Rice:** It offers a supply of complex carbohydrates, crucial for long-term energy. Make sure it is well cooked so that digestion is not an issue.

- **Quinoa:** Complete protein, free of gluten, and high in fiber are some of the benefits. Remember to give it a thorough rinsing to get rid of saponins, which are known to aggravate the digestive system.

- **Sweet Potatoes:** Rich in fiber and vitamins A, C, and B6; low in calories. For improved digestion, make sure you cook the food thoroughly.

- **Oats:** The benefits include being a source of fiber and complex carbs. In order to prevent gastrointestinal distress, slowly introduce the substance.

Vegetables

- **Peas:** An abundance of protein, fiber, vitamins, and minerals are among the benefits. Use in moderation to prevent bloating.

- **Carrots:** The benefits include being a source of vitamins and beta-carotene. Make sure to cook the food properly for optimal digestibility.

- **Green Beans:** It contains a high concentration of vitamins and fiber. To make them simpler to digest, make sure you cook them thoroughly.

- **Zucchini:** The benefits include a strong source of vitamins and minerals, as well as a digestive aid. Cooking the food will improve digestion.

- **Broccoli:** High levels of fiber and vitamins are two of the benefits. To avoid gas, it is important to feed in moderation.

Oils and Fats

- **Olive Oil:** Benefits include providing healthy fats and promoting healthy skin and coat. After cooking, add the ingredients to preserve the nutritional benefits.

- **Flaxseed Oil:** Rich in Omega-3 fatty acids, this product is beneficial to both the health of the heart and the coat. In order to prevent gastrointestinal distress, slowly introduce the substance.

- **Coconut Oil:** Beneficial effects include promoting healthy skin and coats, as well as providing energy. It is important to introduce it gradually.

Extras

- **Cranberries:** Because of its high antioxidant content, it is excellent for the urinary system's health. It is important to introduce it gradually.

General Notes

- Always consult your veterinarian before adding new items to your dog's diet, especially if they have any pre-existing health concerns. This is especially important if your dog has a history of obesity, digestive or bowel problems.

- When introducing new ingredients, it is important to be aware of any adverse reactions your dog may experience. Remember to consult your veterinarian before making any changes to your dog's diet, especially if they have health concerns or dietary restrictions.

- All recipes provide approximately 2–3 servings for average dogs weighing between 20 and 50 pounds, or between 9 and 22.5 kg. For smaller or larger breeds, adjust portions accordingly to ensure they receive the appropriate amount of food based on their specific dietary needs and energy requirements. You should adjust your dog's food intake based on his size and weight, as well as his health condition and activity level, without forgetting that the dog likes to eat.

- Once cooled, store any leftovers in an airtight container in the refrigerator for up to 3 days. For longer storage, portion the food into meal-sized servings and freeze. You can store frozen portions for up to 1 month. Thaw in the refrigerator overnight before serving. Always ensure the food is at room temperature before feeding it to your dog.

Recipe No. 1: Chicken and Rice Delight

Your dog can enjoy a wholesome, balanced meal with Chicken and Rice Delight. It combines high-quality protein from chicken with complex carbohydrates from brown rice, as well as nutrient-rich vegetables like peas and carrots. It's easy to prepare and perfect for dogs of all sizes.

Preparation Time: 30-35 minutes
Type of Cooking: Boiling
Utensils Needed: A pot, knife, chopping board, spoon, and bowl
Difficulty: Easy

Ingredients:

- 1 chicken breast, boneless and skinless: 1 cup (150 g or 0.33 lbs)

- 1 cup of brown rice (190 g or 0.42 lbs)

- 1/2 cup of fresh peas (75 g or 0.16 lbs)

- 1/2 cup of chopped carrots (65 g or 0.14 lbs)

- 1 tablespoon of olive oil (13.5 g or 0.03 lbs)

Instructions:

1. Start by boiling the brown rice in a pot until it's fully cooked, which usually takes about 20 minutes.

2. In a separate pot, boil the chicken breast until it's fully cooked, which should take around 15 minutes.

3. In the last 5 minutes of cooking, add the peas and chopped carrots to the pot alongside the chicken.

4. After cooking everything, drain the water and allow it to cool.

5. Cut the chicken into bite-sized pieces suitable for your dog's size.

6. Combine the chicken, rice, peas, carrots, and olive oil in a bowl. Mix them thoroughly.

7. Serve at room temperature.

Nutritional Values Per Serving:

Protein: 53 g (1.87 oz), Fat: 18 g (0.63 oz), Carbohydrates: 62 g (2.19 oz), Calories: 620 calories.

Health and Allergy Considerations:

This recipe is gluten-free and suitable for dogs with no specific allergies to the ingredients listed. Always consult your vet before introducing new foods into your dog's diet, especially if they have pre-existing health conditions.

Optional Ingredient Substitutions:

If your dog is allergic to chicken, you can substitute it with turkey or cooked salmon. For dogs sensitive to grains, consider using quinoa instead of brown rice.

Concluding Note:

This recipe provides a well-balanced meal for dogs, with chicken as a lean protein source, brown rice for energy, and fresh veggies for fiber and essential vitamins. The inclusion of olive oil makes it ideal for maintaining your dog's energy levels and supporting overall health, including skin and coat condition.

Recipe No. 2: Beef and Veggie Mix

Beef and Veggie Mix combines lean ground beef with nutrient-rich vegetables and flaxseed oil to create a balanced and flavorful meal for your dog. This recipe is especially great for active dogs due to its high protein content and healthy fats.

Preparation Time: 30-35 minutes
Type of Cooking: Boiling and Sautéing
Utensils Needed: Pot, knife, chopping board, spoon, bowl
Difficulty: Easy

Ingredients:

- 1 cup of lean ground beef (225 g or 0.5 lbs)

- 1 cup of cubed sweet potatoes (130 grams or 0.29 lbs)

- 1/2 cup chopped green beans (75 g, or 0.16 lbs)

- 1 tablespoon of flaxseed oil (12 g, or roughly 0.03 lbs)

Instructions:

1. Boil the sweet potatoes in a pot until tender, roughly 15-20 minutes.

2. While the sweet potatoes are boiling, sauté the ground beef in a pan until fully cooked.

3. Add the chopped green beans to the beef and sauté for another 5 minutes.

4. After cooking the beef and green beans and tenderizing the sweet potatoes, remove any excess fat from the beef and remove any water from the potatoes.

5. Combine the beef, green beans, sweet potatoes, and flaxseed oil in a bowl. Mix them well.

6. Let it cool down to room temperature before serving.

Nutritional Values Per Serving:

Protein: 53 g (1.87 oz), Fat: 37 g (1.30 oz), Carbohydrates: 31 g (1.09 oz), Calories: 629 calories.

Health and Allergy Considerations:

Consider potential beef allergies and substitute with another protein if necessary. Sweet potatoes are high in carbohydrates, so use them moderately for overweight dogs. Make sure to thoroughly cook the green beans to facilitate their digestion. Introduce flaxseed oil gradually, especially in dogs with sensitive stomachs. Always consult a veterinarian for tailored advice.

Optional Ingredient Substitutions:

If your dog is sensitive to beef, you can substitute it with turkey or chicken. If flaxseed oil is not available, you can use coconut oil as a healthy alternative that also supports skin and coat health.

Concluding Note:

Ground beef provides essential proteins and amino acids. Sweet potatoes are an excellent source of dietary fiber, vitamins, and minerals. Green beans offer additional fiber and nutrients. Flaxseed oil contributes Omega-3 fatty acids, which can promote a shiny coat and support cognitive function.

We recommend alternating this recipe with other food sources to ensure a complete intake of all necessary nutrients, especially when served regularly.

Recipe No. 3: Salmon, Quinoa, and Vegetable Medley

The Salmon, Quinoa, and Vegetable Medley caters to the health-conscious dog owner who wants to provide their pet with a high-quality, balanced diet. This one-pot recipe is straightforward to prepare and combines salmon, a rich source of Omega-3 fatty acids, with quinoa and vegetables, offering a mix of essential proteins, carbohydrates, and healthy fats.

The simple preparation and fresh ingredients ensure that your dog receives a meal that is not only healthy but also delicious and full of flavor. Perfect for active dogs, this meal supports overall health with a focus on skin, coat, and joint health.

Preparation Time: 35 minutes
Type of Cooking: One-pot Boil
Utensils Needed: Pot, knife, spoon
Difficulty: Easy

Ingredients:

- 1 cup of deboned salmon (300 g or 0.66 lbs), cut into chunks. To ensure safety and quality, it is crucial to remove all bones from fresh salmon

- 1 cup of quinoa (185 g or 0.41 lbs)

- 1/2 cup of green peas (65 g, or 0.14 lbs)

- 1 medium-sized carrot, diced

- 2 cups of water

- 1 tablespoon of olive oil (13.5 g or 0.03 lbs)

Instructions:

1. In a pot, add quinoa and water. Bring it to a boil.

2. Once the quinoa has cooked, reduce the heat and let it simmer for about 15 minutes.

3. Add salmon chunks, green peas, and diced carrots to the pot. Cook the salmon for an additional 5 minutes, or until it reaches the desired doneness.

4. Once cooked, drain excess water and transfer the mixture to a bowl.

5. Drizzle with olive oil, and mix well.

Nutritional Values Per Serving:

Protein: 71 g (2.50 oz), Fat: 37 g (1.30 oz), Carbohydrates: 52 g (1.83 oz), Calories: 858 calories.

Health and Allergy Considerations:

Salmon is excellent for Omega-3 fatty acids, but check for allergies. Quinoa is gluten-free, but ensure it is well-rinsed to remove saponins that can irritate the gut. Peas are rich in protein but can cause bloating in some dogs; use them moderately. Always introduce new foods gradually and consult with a veterinarian to confirm dietary compatibility.

Optional Ingredient Substitutions:

If your dog is sensitive to salmon, you can substitute it with cooked, shredded chicken. For a grain-free option, replace quinoa with a chopped sweet potato (pre-cooked).

Concluding Note:

This Salmon, Quinoa, and Vegetable Medley is not only a delightful meal for your dog but also a powerhouse of nutrition. Salmon provides high-quality protein and essential Omega-3 fatty acids, which are crucial for maintaining healthy skin and joints. Quinoa is a complete protein source and an excellent carbohydrate alternative for energy. Together with peas and carrots, this meal is rich in fiber and vitamins, supporting overall health and vitality.

Recipe No. 4: Turkey and Broccoli Bowl

Turkey and Broccoli Bowl offers a nutritious and satisfying meal for your dog, combining lean protein, fiber, and essential nutrients. This easy-to-prepare recipe uses simple ingredients and cooking techniques that are suitable for any dog owner.

Preparation Time: 25 minutes
Type of Cooking: Boil
Utensils Needed: Pot, knife, spoon
Difficulty: Easy

Ingredients:

- 1 cup of ground turkey (225 g or 0.5 lbs). Ensure the turkey is of good quality and lean to keep the fat content low

- 1/2 cup of finely chopped broccoli florets (45 g or 0.1 lbs). To make broccoli easier for dogs to digest, chop it finely. Broccoli is a good source of fiber and vitamins

- 1/4 cup of rolled oats (25 g or 0.05 lbs). Oatmeal is a good source of complex carbohydrates that can help make a meal more filling and provide sustained energy

- 2 cups of water

Instructions:

1. Start by bringing 2 cups of water to a boil in a pot.

2. Add the ground turkey to the boiling water, breaking it apart with a spoon to ensure even cooking.

3. Once the turkey is halfway cooked (about 5 minutes), add the rolled oats and finely chopped broccoli florets to the pot.

4. Continue to simmer the mixture for an additional 10-15 minutes, or until the turkey is fully cooked and the oats are tender.

5. To avoid a too-watery meal, remove the pot from the heat after cooking everything and carefully drain any excess water.

6. To avoid burning your dog's mouth, allow the mixture to cool to room temperature before serving.

Nutritional Values Per Serving:

Protein: 38 g (1.34 oz), Fat: 11 g (0.39 oz), Carbohydrates: 16 g (0.56 oz), Calories: 313 calories.

Health and Allergy Considerations:

Ground turkey is generally well-tolerated, but ensure it's lean to maintain a low fat content. While broccoli is nutritious, it's important to give it in moderation, as some dogs may experience gas. Oats are good for fiber, but introduce them slowly to avoid gastrointestinal upset. Always consult your veterinarian when introducing new foods to your dog's diet.

Optional Ingredient Substitutions:

For dogs sensitive to turkey, consider using lean cuts of chicken or lamb as a protein alternative. If broccoli's gaseous effects make it unsuitable, consider using spinach or green beans as a less gas-inducing vegetable.

Instead of oats, dogs with grain sensitivities can use cooked sweet potatoes or pumpkin as an alternative carbohydrate source that provides fiber and other nutrients.

Concluding Note:

We designed this Turkey and Broccoli Bowl to offer a balanced meal using high-quality ingredients. Ground turkey is a lean protein source, great for muscle development. Broccoli offers vitamins and minerals, and oats provide a wholesome source of energy without the need for grains that some dogs might be sensitive to.

Recipe No. 5: Chicken and Green Bean Delight

The Chicken & Green Bean Delight recipe combines high-quality chicken protein with fiber-rich green beans and energy-rich brown rice to create a nutritious, balanced meal for your dog.

This simple recipe is easily digestible and perfect for dogs of all sizes, in the right amount for their individual nutritional needs.

Preparation Time: 40 minutes
Type of Cooking: Boiling
Utensils Needed: Pot, knife, spoon, mixing bowl
Difficulty: Easy

Ingredients:

- 1 cup of boiled chicken breast (150 g/0.33 lbs)

- 1 cup of green beans, chopped (150 g/0.33 lbs)

- 1/2 cup of cooked brown rice (125 g/0.275 lbs)

- 1 teaspoon of fish oil

Instructions:

1. Boil the chicken breast until fully cooked. Allow it to cool and then shred it into smaller pieces, which is good for making it easy to digest for dogs.

2. In another pot, boil green beans until they're soft as it makes them easier to digest.

3. Mix the shredded chicken, green beans, and cooked brown rice in a mixing bowl. The brown rice is a good source of complex carbohydrates. Make sure it's cooked until soft.

4. Drizzle fish oil over the mixture and stir. Fish oil is an excellent addition for Omega-3 fatty acids, but ensure the oil is of high quality and suitable for pets. Stirring in the fish oil at the end ensures it retains its nutritional integrity, as Omega-3s can be sensitive to heat.

Nutritional Values Per Serving:

Protein: 50 g (1.76 oz), Fat: 9 g (0.32 oz), Carbohydrates: 36 g (1.27 oz), Calories: 421 calories.

Health and Allergy Considerations:

Ensure the chicken is boneless to prevent choking hazards. Cook the green beans thoroughly to enhance their digestibility. Pets should specifically use fish oil to prevent any harmful additives.

Optional Ingredient Substitutions:

You can substitute turkey or lean pork for dogs sensitive to chicken.

If green beans are not suitable, you can substitute them with zucchini or peas.

You can substitute quinoa or mashed sweet potatoes for dogs with grain sensitivities.

Concluding Note:

This Chicken and Green Bean Delight combines lean protein, fiber, and essential fats, making it ideal for maintaining your dog's energy levels and supporting overall health, including skin and coat condition, thanks to the beneficial effects of Omega-3 fatty acids in fish oil.

Recipe No. 6: Beef and Carrot Casserole

Dogs can enjoy the nutritious and tasty Beef and Carrot Casserole, which combines lean ground beef, fiber-rich carrots, and nutrient-dense peas, all topped with Omega-3-rich flaxseed oil.

Properly portioned, this hearty meal is suitable for dogs of all sizes, especially those with high energy needs.

Preparation Time: 35 minutes
Type of Cooking: Baking
Utensils Needed: Oven, pot, knife, spoon, casserole dish
Difficulty: Moderate

Ingredients:

- 1 cup of ground beef (225 g/0.5 lbs)

- 1 cup of carrots, finely chopped (130 g/0.3 lbs)

- 1/2 cup of peas (75 g/0.165 lbs)

- 1 tablespoon of flaxseed oil (12 g, or roughly 0.03 lbs)

Instructions:

1. Preheat oven to 375°F (190°C).

2. In a pot, cook the ground beef until browned.

3. Add in the chopped carrots and peas and stir until well combined.

4. Transfer to a casserole dish and spread evenly.

5. Bake in oven for about 20 minutes.

6. Before serving, drizzle with flaxseed oil and mix. Adding flaxseed oil after baking is a good strategy to preserve its nutritional benefits, as Omega-3 fatty acids can degrade under high heat.

Nutritional Values Per Serving:

Protein: 54 g (1.90 oz), Fat: 38 g (1.34 oz), Carbohydrates: 23 g (0.81 oz), Calories: 591 calories.

Health and Allergy Considerations:

Ensure the ground beef is lean to avoid excessive fat. This dish is gluten-free and appropriate for dogs without allergies to the ingredients used. Always check with your vet before changing your dog's diet.

Optional Ingredient Substitutions:

If your dog is allergic to beef, you can substitute ground turkey or chicken. If peas are not suitable, you can substitute them with green beans or chopped spinach for similar nutritional benefits. Pumpkin or sweet potatoes are great alternatives to carrots, providing similar textures and nutritional profiles.

Concluding Note:

Diese Beef and Carrot Casserole is a complete meal that provides high-quality protein from beef, while carrots and peas provide essential vitamins and minerals. Flaxseed oil is an excellent source of Omega-3 fatty acids, which are beneficial for heart health and vitality. It's ideal for keeping your dog healthy, active, and satisfied.

Recipe No. 7: Turkey and Sweet Potato Mash

Turkey and Sweet Potato Mash is a wholesome and nutritious option for dogs, combining high-quality protein from turkey with energy-boosting and vitamin-rich sweet potatoes.

Cranberries add a burst of flavor and health benefits, making it a well-rounded dish for your furry friend.

Preparation Time: 45 minutes
Type of Cooking: Boiling
Utensils Needed: A pot, knife, spoon, mixing bowl
Difficulty: Easy

Ingredients:

- 1 cup of ground turkey (225 g/0.5 lbs)

- 1 cup of boiled sweet potato, mashed (200 g/0.44 lbs)

- 1/4 cup of cranberries, finely chopped (40 g/0.088 lbs)

- 1 tablespoon of olive oil (13.5 g or 0.03 lbs)

Instructions:

1. In a pot, cook the ground turkey until fully browned.

2. Prepare the sweet potato puree separately.

3. Mix the mashed sweet potato with the turkey in a mixing bowl.

4. Fold in the chopped cranberries.

5. Drizzle with olive oil and mix until well combined. Drizzling olive oil at the end helps to incorporate healthy fats without cooking them at high temperatures, preserving their benefits.

Nutritional Values Per Serving:

Protein: 37 g (1.30 oz), Fat: 24 g (0.85 oz), Carbohydrates: 56 g (1.98 oz), Calories: 569 calories.

Health and Allergy Considerations:

This recipe is suitable for dogs with no specific allergies to its ingredients. It is gluten-free and uses lean protein and high-fiber vegetables. Always consult your veterinarian before introducing new foods to your dog's diet, especially if they have health conditions or food sensitivities.

Optional Ingredient Substitutions:

If turkey is not suitable, you may substitute it with chicken or even a fish like salmon for a different source of lean protein. If your dog is sensitive to sweet potatoes, butternut squash is a good alternative with similar nutritional benefits. Blueberries can be used instead of cranberries for a similar burst of vitamins and antioxidants. These components will ensure that the recipe is adaptable, safe, and easy to manage, fitting into a variety of dietary plans for different dogs.

Concluding Note:

Turkey is a great choice for lean protein, helping with muscle maintenance. Sweet potatoes, packed with nutrients, promote steady energy release. Cranberries offer additional health benefits, particularly for the urinary tract, making this a balanced and beneficial meal for your dog. Olive oil adds healthy fat and helps in absorbing fat-soluble vitamins.

Recipe No. 8: Salmon and Zucchini Quinoa Bowl

The Salmon & Zucchini Quinoa Bowl provides a nutritious and balanced meal for your dog, combining the high-quality protein of salmon with the wholesome goodness of quinoa and zucchini. It's a light meal that's perfect for dogs who need a nutritious meal without excessive calories.

Preparation Time: 45 minutes
Type of Cooking: Boiling
Utensils Needed: Pot, knife, spoon, mixing bowl
Difficulty: Easy

Ingredients:

- 1 cup of salmon fillet, finely chopped and boneless (225 g/0.5 lbs)

- 1/2 cup of cooked quinoa (85 g/0.19 lbs)

- 1/4 cup of zucchini, diced (40 g/0.088 lbs.)

- 1 teaspoon of coconut oil

Instructions:

1. In a pot, boil the salmon fillet until fully cooked. Let it cool, and then flake it.

2. Mix the cooked quinoa and diced zucchini with the flaked salmon.

3. Drizzle with coconut oil and mix until well combined.

Nutritional Values Per Serving:

Protein: 54 g (1.90 oz), Fat: 31 g (1.09 oz), Carbohydrates: 17 g (0.60 oz), Calories: 533 calories.

Health and Allergy Considerations:

This meal is rich in omega-3 fatty acids and low in allergens. However, it's important to ensure that your dog isn't allergic before introducing salmon. Consult your veterinarian for guidance, especially if your dog has a history of dietary sensitivity.

Optional Ingredient Substitutions:

Cooked chicken or turkey can serve as alternative protein sources for dogs sensitive to salmon. For dogs with grain sensitivities, mashed sweet potato may serve as a carbohydrate alternative, though it alters the texture and nutritional profile of the recipe.

Concluding Note:

Diese Recipe is a simpler, lighter alternative that combines high-quality proteins with essential amino acids from quinoa and the nutritional benefits of zucchini, which aid digestion.

Salmon provides essential proteins and Omega-3 fatty acids, that are beneficial for heart and coat health.

Quinoa is a gluten-free source of carbohydrates and fiber, while zucchini adds vitamins and minerals.

Recipe No. 9: Beef and Carrot Stew

To provide your dog with a hearty and nutritious meal, we have created Beef & Carrot Stew. This recipe combines the high quality protein of beef with the nutritional benefits of carrots and peas, making it ideal for the colder months or as a satisfying comfort meal for your pet.

Preparation Time: 30 minutes
Type of Cooking: Simmering
Utensils Needed: Pot, knife, spoon
Difficulty: Easy

Ingredients:

- 1 cup of lean beef chunks (225 g/0.5 lbs)

- 1 cup of carrots, diced (130 g/0.29 lbs)

- 1/2 cup of peas (72 g/0.16 lbs)

- 2 cups of water or unsalted beef broth. Using unsalted broth keeps the sodium content low, which is healthier for dogs

- 1 tablespoon of olive oil (13.5 g or 0.03 lbs)

Instructions:

1. In a pot, add olive oil and brown the beef chunks.

2. Add carrots, peas, water, or unsalted beef broth.

3. Let simmer for about 20 minutes until the beef is tender and the vegetables are soft.

Nutritional Values Per Serving:

Protein: 58 g (2.05 oz), Fat: 32 g (1.13 oz), Carbohydrates: 24 g (0.85 oz), Calories: 586 calories.

Health and Allergy Considerations:

This stew is gluten-free and low in sodium, making it suitable for dogs with allergies or sensitivities to common food allergens. Always check with your vet before introducing new foods into your dog's diet, especially if they have pre-existing health conditions.

Optional Ingredient Substitutions:

For dogs with a sensitivity to beef, you can substitute it with turkey or chicken. If your dog prefers a different texture or taste, you can substitute pumpkin for carrots.

Concluding Note:

This Beef and Carrot Stew is a wholesome choice that provides a balance of protein, essential fats, and carbohydrates, ideal for supporting your dog's overall health and vitality. It's especially beneficial for active dogs needing high-quality protein for muscle maintenance and repair.

Beef provides essential proteins for muscle growth. Carrots are a source of beta-carotene and vitamins, while peas contain vitamins, minerals, and dietary fiber that aid in digestion.

In the right amount, this recipe is suitable for dogs of all sizes and is a very satisfying and nutritious meal, especially in the colder months.

Recipe No. 10: Fish and Sweet Potato Delight

Fish and Sweet Potato Delight combines high-quality protein from white fish with the wholesome goodness of sweet potatoes and peas to create a nutrient-rich, low-calorie meal for dogs. Dogs who need a diet rich in Omega-3 fatty acids and low in fat can benefit, especially from its simple preparation design.

Preparation Time: 30 minutes
Type of Cooking: Boiling
Utensils Needed: Pot, knife, spoon, mixing bowl
Difficulty: Easy

Ingredients:

- 1 cup of white fish, deboned and finely chopped (225 g/0.5 lbs) White fish is a great low-fat protein source and is also rich in Omega-3 fatty acids, which are beneficial for heart and joint health

- 1/2 cup of sweet potatoes, peeled and chopped (100 g/0.22 lbs) Sweet potatoes are a nutritious, high-fiber carbohydrate source packed with vitamins A, C, and B6

- 1/4 cup of peas (40 g/0.09 lbs) Peas are a good source of vitamins K and B and contain a variety of essential minerals

- 1 tablespoon of olive oil (14 g, or roughly 0.03 lbs) Olive oil is good for your dog's skin and coat health, and it provides essential fatty acids and antioxidants

Instructions:

1. Boil the white fish in a pot until fully cooked. Make sure to remove all the bones to avoid any choking hazards.

2. Boil the chopped sweet potatoes until they are tender.

3. Steam or boil the peas until they are soft.

4. In a mixing bowl, combine the cooked fish, sweet potatoes, and peas.

5. Drizzle with olive oil and stir until everything is evenly mixed.

Nutritional Values Per Serving:

Protein: 30 g (1.06 oz), Fat: 10 g (0.35 oz), Carbohydrates: 25 g (0.88 oz), Calories: 300 calories.

Health and Allergy Considerations:

This meal is free from common allergens such as gluten and is rich in Omega-3 fatty acids, which is beneficial for dogs with joint issues or skin conditions. Consult your vet before introducing new foods into your dog's diet.

Optional Ingredient Substitutions:

Dogs who prefer different tastes or are allergic to fish can substitute the white fish with other lean proteins, such as turkey or rabbit. You can substitute pumpkin for sweet potatoes to achieve a similar texture and nutritional profile.

Concluding Note:

This Fish and Sweet Potato Delight is ideal for maintaining your dog's health with a balance of essential nutrients. It's particularly suitable for older dogs or those with specific dietary needs due to its high Omega-3 content and low-fat profile.

This meal provides lean protein from fish, complex carbohydrates from sweet potatoes, and additional nutrients from peas. Olive oil adds a healthy dose of fats for energy and coat health, making it ideal for dogs that require a diet low in calories but high in essential nutrients and fiber.

Conclusion

Now that we have come to the end of this comprehensive guide, I hope that all my efforts and research have been useful to you. I hope you will use this knowledge in your daily feeding routine. Switching to home-cooked meals, supported by knowledge of what constitutes a balanced and nutritious diet, is an important step in ensuring your dog's long-term health. Remember that every meal you prepare is an expression of your love and commitment to your dog's well-being.

Hearsay and misinformation often obstruct our path to providing the best for our canine companions. Understanding the key aspects of canine nutrition and the intricacies of disease- and breed-specific nutritional requirements is crucial for all dog owners wishing to improve their pet's health through diet.

Together, we have explored the nuances of nutritional management for conditions such as Obesity, Diabetes, and kidney disease. We examined the special needs of puppies, older dogs, and those with chronic conditions such as Osteoarthritis and Cancer. We also used case studies and scientific evidence to expose the dangers hidden in common food ingredients and suggest safer alternatives.

But this book is not the end. Think of it as the beginning of a thorough and ongoing study of your dog's nutrition and health. Remember that the science of dog nutrition is constantly evolving. As new research emerges and our knowledge deepens, it is important to stay informed and adapt our routines to the new findings.

Thank you for embarking on this journey with this dog food guide. So, I invite you to stay in touch, share your experiences, and continue to learn. Your comments, stories, and insights are invaluable to all of us as we strive to provide the best possible care for our furry family members.

Your commitment to your dog's health is a true testament to the incredible bond between humans and their canine companions. Yes, sometimes they are simply better than humans; I know that. If you'd like to get in touch with me, please don't hesitate to contact the editor at *authors@ltpublishing.net*.

I will be happy to answer any questions or concerns you may have. I am also writing a manual on basic dog training, which aims to correct common mistakes and enhance your daily interactions with your dog (I've seen too many mistakes to count). To request advance drafts, contact the publisher.

Additionally, I intend to write a sequel to this manual. If you're interested, you can request a preview at the email address and join our beta readers group, which has early access to my books and can provide valuable feedback.

May you share many happy moments with your beloved canine companion for many years and in good health.

Susan Swanson

From the Same Author

MENTAL EXERCISES FOR DOGS

Unlocking behavior solutions! From misunderstood active dogs to harmonious bonds: Dive into professional training, master the basics, and unlock the secrets of agility!

You can request an excerpt from the book by writing directly to *susan.dog food@ltpublishing.net*

Made in United States
Orlando, FL
11 January 2025